# You Can Stick Your Political Correctness Where the Sun Don't Shine

Written by:
**Alan E Shields**

# INDEX

# Introduction

## *Provocative Insights*

### Unearthing the title's sentiment

The title of this book is not just a mere collection of words intended to grab attention; it serves as a bold declaration of the subject matter that is both urgent and, at times, controversial. Political correctness, while rooted in the admirable goal of ensuring that all individuals are treated with respect and dignity, has now morphed into a tool that often suppresses free speech, encourages self-censorship, and sometimes, ironically, perpetuates the very prejudices it aims to combat.

Consider, for instance, the instance of a university professor being reprimanded for using an age-old idiom that was misconstrued as offensive, even though its origin had nothing to do with the perceived slight. Such instances, unfortunately, are not isolated. They underscore a larger cultural phenomenon where the fear of offending has become paralyzing, inhibiting genuine interactions and open discourse.

The title, thus, is a call to delve deep into this phenomenon, to question the direction our society is heading in, and to ask the hard questions: Is our pursuit of absolute political correctness leading to a more understanding society, or is it pushing us further apart?

### The rise of the anti-PC sentiment

Parallel to the ascent of hyper-political correctness, there has been a countermovement, a rising sentiment against what many perceive as 'PC gone mad.' This isn't simply a reactionary backlash from those unwilling to adapt to changing societal norms. It's more nuanced, driven by individuals from various backgrounds who believe that the essence of political correctness is being lost in its current overzealous application.

For instance, well-known comedians like John Cleese and Jerry Seinfeld have voiced concerns over performing on college campuses, a space once celebrated for fostering free thought and expression. Their reasons? The fear of unintentional offense leading to disproportionate backlash. Such sentiments from renowned figures are symptomatic of a broader societal concern: that political correctness is stifling the very creativity and discourse it was meant to protect.

Moreover, the rise of this anti-PC sentiment is also indicative of a society that feels increasingly polarized. Many are growing frustrated, feeling as if they're constantly navigating a minefield of potential offenses, unable to express genuine questions or concerns without the looming threat of public castigation.

**The cultural shift that necessitated the book's conception**

The cultural landscape of the 21st century is markedly different from any other time in history. Rapid advancements in technology, especially the rise of social media, have connected us in unprecedented ways. This hyper-connectedness, while boasting numerous advantages, has also given rise to a culture of instant outrage, where individuals or groups can be 'canceled' based on perceived slights, often without a comprehensive understanding of context.

Take the fictional case of Anna, a renowned author who, in her earlier works, explored themes that, by today's standards, could be considered controversial. Without considering the context of the time when she wrote these pieces or her intentions behind them, a Twitter mob calls for her books to be banned. Anna's lifetime of work, the nuances of her narratives, and her contributions to literature are suddenly at risk of being overshadowed by decontextualized snippets from her past works.

Such cultural shifts, where judgments are swift and often absolute, necessitate a deep dive into the phenomenon of political correctness. This book, therefore, is an attempt to understand, critique, and offer insights into a world where the line between genuine respect for individual rights and the suppression of free discourse seems increasingly blurred.

## *Mapping the Terrain:*
## *Capturing the omnipresent influence of political correctness*

### The Pervasiveness of Political Correctness

Political correctness, in the beginning, was a force for good. It sought to address genuine issues of discrimination, prejudice, and bias by advocating for a more inclusive language. Over the years, however, it has morphed into something far more encompassing. Now, it's omnipresent, influencing everything from pop culture to politics, academia to advertising. Some could argue that the seeds of political correctness have now rooted themselves into the very fabric of our lives, subtly dictating our words, thoughts, and actions. For instance, movies from the 80s and 90s, once considered humorous and lighthearted, are now scrutinized, with many scenes branded as problematic. The question arises: are we being cautious, or are we being too oversensitive? Answer: Way too oversensitive.

### Recognizing Its Influence in Daily Life

The reach of political correctness isn't confined to high-profile incidents or public figures; it impacts the daily lives of regular people. Conversations at the dinner table, discussions in classrooms, or casual banter at workplaces have all been touched by the heavy hand of PC culture. One cannot overlook the hesitations, the paused moments before speaking, or the overthinking that follows a seemingly innocent remark, for fear of unintentional offense. Consider, for example, the hesitation of a teacher who refrains from discussing a historically accurate event because it might upset someone. Or, take the case of a coworker who avoids making a cultural reference in casual conversation for fear of being labeled ignorant, a bigot, or worse, a racist. These micro-moments in daily life highlight the pervasive nature of political correctness and its power to stifle spontaneous expression.

## The Transformation from a Social Guideline to a Societal Mandate

Initially, political correctness was a guiding principle. It was a roadmap to navigate the complexities of an increasingly diverse society. Its aim was noble: reduce harm, increase understanding, and promote coexistence. Yet, as it evolved, the lines blurred between being a mere guideline and a strict code of conduct, a transformation that has been both rapid and profound. Over time, what started as suggestions for considerate communication became unwritten laws, with breaches often leading to social ostracization. A fitting example is the rise of cancel culture, where a single misstep, sometimes from years past, can ruin careers and reputations overnight. In many ways, political correctness no longer feels like a tool for unity and understanding; it feels more like a weapon, wielded by some to suppress, and dominate others. The transformation is evident: from being a social compass, it has turned into a societal mandate with its own set of consequences.

## *The Catalyst: The Spark That Ignites Discontent*

### Personal Encounters with Stifled Speech

For many individuals, the constraints of political correctness are not just theoretical discussions debated in academic circles or dissected in newsroom debates. They are real, tangible encounters that affect personal freedoms, livelihoods, and mental well-being. Consider John, a college professor, who hesitates to discuss certain topics in his sociology class, fearing backlash from students or administration. His expertise lies in exploring societal shifts and trends, but he finds himself self-censoring to avoid potential pitfalls of political correctness. Or, consider the case of Sarah, a novelist, who ditches a character from her book because she worries it might be perceived as a stereotype, even though it's based on a real person she knew. Such personal encounters highlight how the tentacles of PC culture have infiltrated private spaces, dictating not only what people say but also what they think, stunting creative processes, and often leading to self-imposed silence.

## The Notable Public Incidents that Scream Suppression

The public sphere, with its ever-watchful eye, has been rife with incidents that underscore the suppressive nature of political correctness. High-profile figures, from comedians to politicians, have felt its burn. A notable example is Kevin Hart, a comedian who faced immense backlash for tweets he posted almost a decade ago, leading to his withdrawal from hosting the Oscars. While only a few argue that such reactions are necessary for accountability, most others think that digging up past mistakes, especially when acknowledged and apologized for, does not serve justice, it merely satisfies the hunger of an outraged mob. Another instance is J.K. Rowling, the famous author, who faced intense criticism for expressing her views on gender and sex. The widespread condemnation and calls for book boycotts raised concerns: we are clearly not in a society that encourages open dialogue. We are slowly inching towards a space where only select voices are deemed acceptable, which in itself, is unacceptable.

## The Collective Societal Response and Its Implications

The societal response to political correctness is far from uniform. While many champion it as a necessary evolution towards a more inclusive society, most people feel stifled, silenced, and even resentful. This division is evident in the rise of movements that push back against PC culture. A prominent example is the intellectual dark web, a group of academics, writers, and thinkers who challenge the mainstream narrative and advocate for open dialogue. Their rising popularity indicates a hunger for spaces free from the confines of political correctness. Moreover, the election of figures who openly mock or challenge PC norms reflects a collective frustration. When significant sections of society feel unheard or marginalized, it can have severe implications, fostering resentment, amplifying division, and even affecting electoral outcomes. The backlash against political correctness, in many ways, isn't just about language or sensitivity. It's a reflection of deeper societal fractures, underscoring the need for a balanced approach.

## *The Consequences of Silence: The Price of Muted Conversations*

### The Dangers of Muffled Voices

In an age where communication has become more accessible than ever, ironically, many find themselves silenced by the looming shadow of political correctness. When individuals fear expressing their views, it leads to a stifling of creativity, innovation, and personal growth. Muffled voices often resort to echo chambers where their beliefs are rarely challenged, leading to a reinforcement of potentially misguided notions. For instance, a journalist who refrains from covering a story from a particular angle due to the fear of backlash isn't just compromising on journalistic integrity but is also withholding vital perspectives from the public discourse. Another case can be made for scientists and researchers who, fearing public outrage, might shy away from pursuing certain studies or publishing results that could be perceived as controversial, thus hampering the progress of knowledge.

### The Societal Cost of Not Fostering Open Dialogue

When societies fail to foster open dialogue, they inadvertently cultivate an environment of suspicion and mistrust. The free exchange of ideas, once the cornerstone of progressive societies, starts to wane, replaced by homogeneous thinking. This lack of diversity in thought has long-term repercussions. It hinders problem-solving, as potential solutions are dismissed without discussion, and discourages younger generations from critical thinking. A pertinent example of this can be observed in university campuses, historically the bastions of free thought. In recent years, there have been instances of invited speakers being disinvited or shouted down because their views were deemed "unacceptable." Such environments not only deprive students of a holistic education but also send a message: dissent is not welcome. This breeds a generation less equipped to handle differing opinions and more prone to confirmation bias.

## The Undermining of Fundamental Democratic Values

Democracies thrive on the pillars of free speech, open dialogue, and the right to dissent. However, when political correctness dictates what can and cannot be said, these pillars are eroded. The very essence of a democratic society is the belief that every individual has a voice, and every voice matters. However, when voices are silenced in the name of avoiding offense, it undermines this foundational principle. There's a growing concern that in the pursuit of not offending anyone, societies might be sacrificing the democratic values that champion the rights of the individual. A case in point is the legal battles faced by bakers who, based on personal beliefs, declined to make custom wedding cakes for same-sex couples. Whether one agrees with their stance or not, the incident raises a significant question: At what point does the enforcement of political correctness infringe upon individual rights and freedom of expression? The delicate balance between collective sensitivity and individual rights becomes paramount in preserving the essence of democratic societies.

## *The Question of Intent:*
## *Reading Between the Lines or Overanalyzing Them?*

### Delving into the Purpose Behind Words

Language is a nuanced tool, and its interpretation can significantly vary based on context, tone, cultural background, and individual experiences. At its core, intent governs the message a speaker wishes to convey. In casual conversations, friends might jest or use words colloquially without meaning harm. Comedians, for instance, often push boundaries to make audiences think or to satirize societal norms. In a world before the stranglehold of excessive political correctness, there was room for such exchanges, and the onus was on listeners to discern intent. However, the shift towards extreme political correctness has pivoted the focus from "what is being said" to "how it might be perceived," regardless of the speaker's original intention. This change forces individuals to be overly cautious, often diluting authentic communication and depriving conversations of depth and candor.

## Instances Where Intent Was Grossly Misinterpreted

Instances Where Intent Was Grossly Misinterpreted The landscape of public discourse is littered with instances where well-intentioned comments were blown out of proportion due to misinterpretation. Take, for example, a professor who uses a historical term in its correct context during a lecture but faces backlash for its contemporary controversial connotations. Or the case of Sir Tim Hunt, a Nobel laureate, who made a comment about the "trouble with girls" in labs during a conference. Though he later clarified that he was being ironic and supportive of female scientists, his words were taken at face value, leading to severe backlash and his eventual resignation from an honorary position. Such examples underscore the dangers of prioritizing perceived sentiment over the actual intent behind words, often leading to undue vilification.

## The Dangers of an Overly Analytical Approach to Everyday Dialogue

Obsessing over every word and its possible interpretations can transform everyday dialogues into minefields. When individuals constantly second-guess their words, fearful of unintentional slights, it restricts fluid conversation. This hyper-analytical approach can strain personal relationships, as friends and family may become wary of open communication to avoid potential misunderstandings. On a broader scale, it can stifle journalistic freedom, artistic expression, and even academic discourse. For instance, authors might avoid exploring certain themes or characters in their work, fearing backlash, despite their intention being to shed light on these issues. This overly analytical lens also fosters a society where individuals are perpetually on the defense, ready to justify their words and actions constantly. The richness of spontaneous, heartfelt communication is lost, replaced by rehearsed, sanitized dialogues that barely scratch the surface of genuine human interaction.

## *A World on Eggshells: Tiptoeing Through Conversations*

### The Anxiety Surrounding Daily Interactions

In today's climate of excessive political correctness, there's a palpable tension that envelopes daily interactions. From office water cooler chats to casual banter at family gatherings, there's a hovering fear of inadvertently saying something "wrong" or "offensive." This isn't merely about avoiding explicit slurs or derogatory comments, which should undeniably be condemned. It's about the anxiety stemming from the potential misinterpretation of innocent remarks. For instance, a simple compliment about someone's attire or hairstyle might be misconstrued as a comment laden with racial or gender biases. Such an environment fosters self-doubt and apprehension. Instead of cherishing human connections and the joy of sharing, individuals find themselves meticulously filtering their words, leading to stilted and strained interactions.

### The Rise of Rehearsed, Insincere Communication

To navigate this minefield of potential misinterpretations, many have turned to rehearsed, tried-and-tested modes of communication. This is particularly evident in public figures, corporate leaders, and even educators who, wary of backlash, often resort to "safe" scripts. Instead of spontaneous responses, there's an increased reliance on pre-approved statements, often crafted by PR teams or legal departments. The spontaneity of dialogues at panel discussions or interviews is replaced by predictable, sterilized answers. This not only dulls the essence of dynamic interactions but also breeds insincerity. For instance, after a corporate misstep, how often have we seen CEOs issue eerily similar apologies, laden with buzzwords but devoid of genuine remorse or commitment to change?

**The Loss of Genuine, Heartfelt Conversation**

One of the gravest casualties of this hyper-politically correct world is the demise of genuine, from-the-heart conversations. When individuals are perpetually wary of being judged or misconstrued, they're less likely to share personal anecdotes, experiences, or insights. Such reservations hinder the blossoming of deep connections. For example, an individual might refrain from discussing their cultural traditions or unique upbringing, fearing it might be deemed "exotic" or "different" in a negative light. Or consider the hesitant parent, unsure of how to approach a topic about diverse families at their child's school, opting for vagueness over a potentially enriching dialogue. These missed opportunities for deeper understanding and connection only widen the chasm of misunderstanding, leaving society more polarized and less empathetic.

## *Peering Ahead: Embarking on a Journey of Understanding*

**A Preview of the Explorations in the Upcoming Chapters**

As we venture further into this exploration of political correctness, readers will be introduced to a myriad of themes, shedding light on the intricate web that PC has woven into our daily lives. The forthcoming chapters will take an incisive look into how artists have had to modify their expressions in the name of political correctness, often at the altar of their artistic vision. We'll delve into the international perceptions of PC, revealing that this isn't merely a Western phenomenon but a global sentiment with varying degrees of resonance. On the one hand, there are genuine grievances and attempts at creating a more inclusive society, but on the other, there are many cases of overreach that have left individuals feeling marginalized in the very efforts aimed at inclusion.

**What Readers Can Expect in the Subsequent Discourse**

Beyond just broad themes, readers should anticipate detailed case studies, firsthand accounts, and a rich tapestry of examples that bring to life the arguments presented. One could expect a deep dive into the university campuses – once hailed as bastions of free thought – now grappling with the conundrum of ensuring safe spaces while preserving academic freedom. Furthermore, the contentious issue of representation in media, especially concerning the LGBTQ+ community, will be scrutinized, presenting instances where political correctness overstepped its mark, leading to misrepresentation rather than genuine inclusion. We'll also take a critical look at sports, focusing on the intricate debate surrounding transgender women's participation in women's sports. Through these discussions, readers will be equipped with a nuanced perspective on political correctness, one that acknowledges its merits but remains wary of its excesses.

**Setting the Stage for a Deep Dive into Political Correctness**

In this book, I, as the author, will focus primarily on the negative aspects of political correctness. While acknowledging the well-intentioned roots of the concept, I'll delve into its excesses and the challenges it poses to open discourse. As we navigate through, readers will be encouraged to differentiate between authentic inclusivity efforts and situations where political correctness might suppress genuine dialogue or differing opinions. The journey ahead might be unsettling at times, but it's only through such rigorous scrutiny that we can hope to find a way out. By the conclusion, my aspiration is that readers will possess not only a refined understanding of political correctness but also a perspective to foster healthier, more balanced discussions about its place in our world.

# Chapter 1
# The Rise of Political Correctness

## *PC's Dubious Roots: Tracing the Path of Political Correctness*

### Differentiating Noble Pursuits from Divisive Agendas

While the initial impetus for many of these movements was undeniably noble – advocating for justice, equality, and a voice for the marginalized – there emerged a more pernicious side. For instance, within university campuses, spaces that should champion free thought and intellectual rigor, there grew an increasing intolerance for contrarian views in the name of being "politically correct." It's vital to recognize that the overarching objectives of these movements, like racial equality or women's rights, were essential societal goals. However, the means employed to achieve these ends started to become questionable. One notable incident from recent history would be the case of a Yale professor who faced backlash for merely suggesting students should be allowed to choose their Halloween costumes, even if they might be seen as culturally insensitive. While her intent was to advocate for a space where young adults could make their own decisions (and face the consequences of those choices), she was vilified for promoting "insensitivity."

### The Transformation from Civil Rights Dialogues to a Broader Societal Approach

Over time, what began as focused dialogues around civil rights began to bleed into broader societal discourses. While initially, political correctness sought to challenge derogatory terms or phrases that perpetuated stereotypes or prejudice, its scope expanded dramatically. Now, it wasn't just about changing certain words but about altering entire narratives. Industries, especially entertainment and media, were among the first to feel this seismic shift. Movies and television shows began receiving criticism for storylines or characters that didn't fit the "politically correct" mold. For instance, classic movies from Hollywood's Golden Age have come under scrutiny for their depiction of gender roles or racial stereotypes. While it's essential to analyze and understand historical content with a modern perspective, it's also crucial to acknowledge the context in which they were created. Instead of serving as platforms for open discussion and critical analysis, many of these forums morphed into arenas of overt sensitivity, sometimes bordering on censorship, where content was analyzed not for its artistic or historical merit, but solely through the lens of modern-day political correctness.

## *Society's PC Embrace: The Grip Tightens*

### The World's Shrinking: Global Communication and the Need for a Unified Language That Does Not Stifle Free Speech

In the age of globalization, rapid technological advances, and the ever-increasing dominance of the Internet, the world has become a more connected space. This has led to a blending of cultures, ideas, and dialogues on a previously unparalleled scale. Communication platforms such as social media, news outlets with global reach, and online forums enable interactions across continents in real-time. Given the vast cultural and linguistic diversity, there emerged an implicit need for a "universal" language or a set of guidelines that could be understood and adhered to globally. Enter political correctness, which, in many ways, seemed to offer an answer by providing a "safe" framework for international communication. However, the pitfalls became apparent quickly. The free exchange of ideas, a cornerstone of democratic values, faced an increasing threat. An example that springs to mind is the global tech companies that began to implement community standards or guidelines to moderate content on their platforms. While the intent was to foster respectful interactions, they inadvertently created environments where users feared retribution for voicing unpopular opinions.

## Political Correctness as a False Bridge Between Diverse Cultures

With the noble intention of creating harmonious dialogue between various cultures, political correctness positioned itself as the bridge connecting these worlds. The premise was simple: if everyone adhered to a universally accepted set of guidelines in communication, cultural clashes could be minimized. Yet, as time unfolded, this bridge began to resemble a precarious tightrope more than a sturdy passageway. Instead of promoting genuine understanding and appreciation, political correctness often acted as a superficial band-aid, hiding underlying prejudices or misunderstandings. For example, in multinational corporations, employees might undergo training sessions on cultural sensitivity. Still, these often ended up as checkbox exercises, where participants learned what not to say rather than genuinely understanding and valuing diverse perspectives.

## The Potential Overshadowing of Individual Cultural Nuances

One of the unintended consequences of the global adoption of political correctness was the potential erasure or dilution of individual cultural nuances. As societies strove for a unified language of respect, subtleties unique to each culture were sometimes overshadowed by broad generalizations. For instance, in a bid to avoid cultural appropriation or to demonstrate respect, certain festivals or traditions were "sanitized" for global consumption, often losing their original essence in the process. A fitting example is the western adaptation of yoga. What began as a profound spiritual discipline in ancient India has, in some western contexts, been reduced to mere physical exercise, stripped of its philosophical and meditative aspects. While it's essential to adapt practices to fit different cultural contexts, the line between adaptation and oversimplification, or even misrepresentation, is a thin one. This oversimplification, often a result of trying to be "politically correct," risks losing the rich tapestry of cultural diversity that makes our global society so vibrant.

## *The Downward Spiral: From Idealism to Suppression*

**The Emerging Negatives of Political Correctness**

Political correctness promised a more inclusive, sensitive, and respectful societal landscape, especially in discourse. But as the saying goes, the road to hell is often paved with good intentions. With time, the demand for a meticulously sanitized language began to outweigh the initial motives. The very tool that aimed to eradicate insensitivity began to fan the flames of polarization. Many felt that it began to stifle genuine self-expression, making individuals overly cautious about every word they uttered or wrote. Beyond that, it inadvertently fostered resentment. Individuals who might have inadvertently used a term that was now considered "incorrect" often faced public shaming or ostracization. Instead of fostering an environment of education and growth, the culture of political correctness at times mutated into one of intimidation and fear.

**Case Studies: Early Instances of Artists, Academics, and Commoners Feeling Suppressed**

As political correctness became more pervasive, numerous public figures, especially artists and academics, found themselves at the epicenter of controversy. For instance, consider the case of a renowned university professor who faced intense backlash for questioning the practice of using gender-neutral pronouns. While his intention was to spark a philosophical discussion on language's evolution, he was quickly labeled a bigot, and calls for his termination echoed across the academic community. Artists, too, felt the pinch. Many comedians, musicians, and filmmakers began to second-guess their creative choices, fearful of provoking outrage. One notable example is a famous comedian who, in the mid-2010s, faced significant backlash for a joke deemed insensitive. While the comedian believed in comedy's role as a societal mirror, reflecting both the good and the bad, many saw it as a blatant disregard for the feelings of marginalized groups. This growing climate of fear had profound implications, not just for public figures but for everyday people.

Discussions around family dinner tables, in college classrooms, or at local pubs began to be colored with caution, as individuals feared being misinterpreted or labeled intolerant.

**The Query of Whether Society Saw It Coming**

In retrospect, the question arises: Could society have anticipated the downsides of political correctness? Were there warning signs that this noble pursuit was veering into suppressive territory? Many argue that the warning bells were ringing loud and clear, but collective denial and the fear of going against the popular narrative drowned them out. Others opine that the rapid spread of social media, which allowed for instantaneous and often anonymous judgment, exacerbated the issue. These platforms provided a megaphone to the loudest voices, often overshadowing nuanced discussions. Furthermore, the rise of "cancel culture," where individuals faced swift and often disproportional retribution for perceived wrongs, became a testament to the pitfalls of unchecked political correctness. Yet, despite these signs, many segments of society chose to embrace this trend wholeheartedly, driven by a genuine desire to make the world a more inclusive place. The challenge, however, lay in discerning genuine inclusivity from the superficial, and often suppressive, varnish of political correctness.

## *Clashing Intents and Interpretations: The Turbulent Terrain of Language and Meaning*

**Instances Where Words Were Misconstrued**

The human lexicon is a tapestry woven with various threads of intent, tone, cultural background, and context. Given its complexity, it is unsurprising that many words or statements are susceptible to misinterpretation. Yet, with the rise of political correctness, such misinterpretations often have grave ramifications. An illustrative case is that of a renowned author who, during a press interview, spoke about the importance of cultural exchange. The author used a proverb from their native culture to underscore the message. However, many who heard or read the comment perceived it as an act of cultural appropriation. Instead of viewing it as a nod to the richness of the author's own heritage, they interpreted it as a casual theft of another culture. The author faced immense backlash and was pressured into issuing a public apology. Such instances underline the challenges posed by political correctness, where the chasm between intent and interpretation often widens unpredictably.

## The Subjective Nature of Offense

"Offense is taken, not given," is a saying that holds profound implications in the realm of political correctness. What might seem benign or even complimentary to one individual can be deeply offensive to another. This subjectivity makes navigating the landscape of communication akin to traversing a minefield. For example, in many cultures, commenting on someone's weight or appearance is considered a gesture of familiarity or concern. Yet, in more politically correct climates, such remarks are often seen as invasive or even derogatory. A well-intentioned compliment about someone's "exotic" looks can be perceived as othering or stereotyping. The challenge lies in the fact that offense is deeply personal and varies from individual to individual. While political correctness seeks to offer a one-size-fits-all solution to avoid offense, the diverse tapestry of human emotions and perceptions often resists such simplification.

## Personal Biases and Their Role in Perception

Personal biases, shaped by individual experiences, cultural backgrounds, and societal influences, play a pivotal role in how words are perceived. With the rise of political correctness, these biases often come to the forefront, coloring interpretations and guiding reactions. A statement that aligns with an individual's deeply held beliefs or experiences might be lauded, while another that clashes might be condemned. For instance, an academic paper that critiques certain aspects of modern feminism might be labeled regressive or even misogynistic, not necessarily based on its merit or arguments but based on the inherent biases of the readers. The same paper, when read by someone with a different set of biases, might be hailed as a necessary critique. This divergence in perceptions underscores the challenges of striving for objective interpretations in a world deeply influenced by subjective biases. Political correctness, in its attempt to streamline communication and make it universally palatable, often struggles against these ingrained biases, leading to clashes, misunderstandings, and, at times, unwarranted vilification.

## *Misusing the PC Banner:*
## *From Noble Pursuits to Ulterior Motives*

### Recognizing the Weaponization of Political Correctness

The essence of political correctness aimed to bridge gaps, to allow for the representation of marginalized voices, and to counteract prejudiced or harmful rhetoric. However, like many tools designed for benevolent purposes, political correctness has been hijacked and weaponized. There have been situations where the umbrella of "PC" is wielded not as a shield to protect the vulnerable, but as a sword to attack opponents. The fear of being labeled "politically incorrect" can stifle open discourse, as individuals become wary of speaking lest they inadvertently transgress an ever-shifting line. In the public sphere, such weaponization can be particularly damaging. Figures, especially those in the limelight, might be held hostage to these standards, often facing undue criticism or calls for cancellations based on minor infractions or even well-intentioned comments.

### Cases Where PC Was Used More for Personal Vendetta Than Genuine Concern

Underneath the lofty ideals of political correctness, there have been murky waters where individuals exploit its principles for personal gains or vendettas. An example that springs to mind is that of a university professor who faced accusations of perpetuating stereotypes in a literary analysis class. A student, bearing a personal grudge against the professor due to unrelated circumstances, began a campaign accusing the educator of racial insensitivity. The claims, though largely unfounded and taken out of context, gained traction among peers who were unfamiliar with the full story. The professor, despite years of dedication to fostering inclusive education, found themselves at the center of a storm, facing disciplinary actions and public disgrace. This incident, among others, raises questions about the ease with which the banner of political correctness can be misused, leading to unwarranted consequences for individuals who are innocent of the charges levied against them.

**Differentiating Sincere PC Advocacies from Manipulative Ones**

One of the most pressing challenges in today's age of rapid information dissemination is discerning genuine advocacies from manipulative ones. When every call-out or accusation carries the potential to go viral, how does one sift through the noise to identify legitimate concerns? True advocates for political correctness often come from a place of wanting to uplift marginalized communities, educate the masses, and create a more harmonious society. Their efforts are characterized by constructive dialogues, educational initiatives, and a willingness to listen and adapt. In contrast, manipulative advocacies often exhibit traits of hostility, refusal to engage in open dialogue, and a tendency to jump to conclusions without a comprehensive understanding of context. Moreover, these insincere campaigns might focus more on punitive measures—like "canceling" individuals—rather than fostering understanding and growth. Differentiating between these two can be challenging, but it is imperative to ensure that the base principles of political correctness are upheld without descending into avenues of personal vendettas or manipulative agendas.

## *The Global Perspective: A Mosaic of PC Interpretations*

### How Political Correctness Evolved Differently Across the World

Political correctness, though it often feels like a Western-centric concept, has roots and manifestations across the globe, but its manifestation differs substantially depending on regional historical, cultural, and socio-political factors. For instance, in Latin America, political correctness has intertwined closely with efforts to combat the lingering impacts of colonialism and to recognize the rights and identities of indigenous populations. In post-apartheid South Africa, the concept is intricately linked with reconciling a harrowing history of racial segregation and working towards genuine integration. Meanwhile, in parts of the Middle East, political correctness might pivot more towards religious and social decorum, respecting the intricacies of tribal and religious dynamics.

### Contrasting the West's PC Evolution with that of the East

The West, especially North America and Europe, has seen political correctness develop primarily in tandem with issues related to race, gender, sexuality, and more recently, concerns about colonialism and historical revisionism. The rise of multiculturalism, especially in urban centers, has amplified discussions on inclusivity and representation. For instance, debates about representation in Hollywood or the renaming of institutions that carry colonial or racist legacies are quintessentially Western PC concerns.

Contrast this with the East, where the narrative is substantially different. In countries like China, political correctness might revolve around issues of regionalism, Han centrality, and, to an extent, the recognition of its many ethnic minorities. Japan, with its history of imperial expansion and wartime actions, faces its own unique PC challenges, especially relating to its interactions with neighboring countries and the narrative taught in its schools. In India, a nation of profound diversity, political correctness addresses the challenges of caste, religion, and linguistic differences. It's essential to understand that what might be deemed "politically correct" in a Western nation could be entirely different in the East due to the differing historical and cultural contexts.

## Identifying Cultural Elements that Shape a Nation's PC Narrative

The cultural fabric of a nation greatly determines how political correctness is perceived and practiced. For instance, nations with a collectivist culture, such as many in Asia, might prioritize harmony and societal stability over individual expression, which can lead to a different type of self-censorship where controversial topics might be avoided to maintain societal equilibrium. On the other hand, individualistic societies, like the U.S., may place a higher premium on personal expression, leading to more public and vibrant debates about what constitutes "correctness."

Furthermore, the historical context cannot be separated from the PC narrative. Countries that have undergone colonial subjugation, such as many African and Asian nations, often have political correctness issues related to their colonial past, post-colonial identity, and the legacies of historical injustices. Contrastingly, countries that were colonizers may face PC challenges in acknowledging past misdeeds and addressing contemporary implications of their historical actions.

In conclusion, while political correctness is a global phenomenon, its specifics are intensely local, shaped by the intricate dance of history, culture, and socio-political dynamics of each region.

## *Setting the Future Stage:*
## *The Echoes of PC's Infancy in Contemporary Times*

### The Impact of the Early Days of PC on Modern Discourse

The embryonic days of political correctness have left undeniable marks on our modern discourse. During its inception, the goals of PC were laudable: promoting sensitivity, understanding, and respect for all, irrespective of their backgrounds. Yet, as it evolved, the rigidity with which some of its principles were enforced created a kind of linguistic and thought straitjacket. For instance, in academia, some scholars began to feel the pressure to produce work that was politically correct rather than intellectually honest. An example can be seen in some debates surrounding ancient civilizations. Some historians felt pressured to underplay the transgressions of certain cultures or civilizations to make their narrative more palatable to modern sensibilities, even if it meant sacrificing historical accuracy.

**Recognizing the Brewing Storm**

Behind the polished facade of early political correctness, there was a storm gathering, a looming conflict between those who championed unrestricted free speech and those who believed that certain sentiments should be suppressed for the greater good. This dichotomy was not just a debate of semantics but a clash of ideologies. The ideal of preventing harm and promoting inclusivity was beginning to clash with the preservation of genuine, unfiltered dialogue. An illustrative case of this brewing tension was the controversy surrounding Salman Rushdie's novel "The Satanic Verses." While the book was a work of fiction, it drew anger from many in the Muslim community, leading to Rushdie receiving death threats and living in hiding. The incident highlighted a growing global contention: where should the line be drawn between freedom of expression and respect for religious and cultural sensitivities?

**Preparing Readers for a Journey into the Deeper Waters of PC Controversies**

As we delve further into the complexities of political correctness in the subsequent chapters, readers should brace themselves for a journey into often tumultuous waters. These aren't just debates about choosing the right words; they are battles over foundational principles that underlie the societies we've built. How do we strike a balance between preventing "hate" speech and preserving freedom of speech? Is it possible to ensure no one is ever offended while still upholding the tenets of open dialogue and honest discussion? Of course not! While the early days of PC sowed the seeds of these debates, the controversies have grown, evolved, and taken on new dimensions in our modern age. As we move forward, we will explore how political correctness has influenced media, academia, politics, and even personal relationships, shedding light on its multifaceted impact on our world.

# Chapter 2
# Muzzling the Masses

## *The Free Speech Sacrifice:*
## *When Silence Drowns Out the Din of Discussion*

### How Political Correctness Began Overshadowing the Right to Expression

The principle of free speech, enshrined in many constitutions and revered as a foundational tenet of democracies, found itself increasingly stifled as political correctness began to spread its influence. Initially, as with many well-intended concepts, its application began to veer into extremes. Suddenly, it wasn't just about avoiding blatant slurs or promoting understanding. It started to include avoiding any topic that might be deemed controversial or that could potentially offend someone, somewhere. This led to a kind of self-censorship, where individuals would refrain from speaking out of fear, not out of respect. A palpable example of this could be found on college campuses, traditionally bastions of free thought and debate. Here, speakers were sometimes disinvited or shouted down because their viewpoints didn't align with a certain accepted narrative, illustrating a stark departure from the open dialogue universities were supposed to champion.

### Recognizing the Cost of Silence: The Societal Implications of Suppressed Voices

The ramifications of muting voices under the banner of political correctness are manifold and deeply entrenched within the societal fabric. At its core, the act of silencing discourages diversity of thought. It creates an echo chamber where only one "correct" perspective is amplified, leading to intellectual stagnation. Furthermore, the fear of reprisal means that genuine issues might never come to light. If individuals are afraid of the backlash they might face for bringing up contentious topics, those topics remain undiscussed and unresolved. This also engenders resentment, as people feel that their fundamental rights are being curtailed. An anecdotal reflection of this is seen in the surge of underground forums and websites that cater to "free thinkers" or those who feel marginalized by mainstream discourse. While some of these platforms host genuine discussions, others have become hotbeds for extremism, proving that when voices are suppressed in the mainstream, they often find outlets in the shadows, sometimes with dire consequences.

## Silencing Dissent:
## When Creative Minds Are Bound by Invisible Chains

### Artists, Authors, and Thinkers: The Frontline Warriors

Artists, authors, and thinkers have historically been society's mirrors, reflecting its virtues, vices, and evolving dynamics. They play a pivotal role in shaping societal thought and pushing boundaries, often questioning norms and challenging status quos. However, with the rise of political correctness, these very individuals—once celebrated for their boldness and vision—found themselves on the frontline, battling accusations of insensitivity, bigotry, or worse. Their art, meant to provoke thought or present a different perspective, was increasingly scrutinized for not aligning with the rapidly narrowing confines of 'acceptable' discourse. A notable manifestation of this was in the film industry, where filmmakers had to tread lightly to avoid offending any group. Movies that aimed to critique or satirize certain aspects of society were met with backlash even before they were released, leading many to question whether artistic freedom was becoming a relic of the past.

### Notable Figures Who Experienced Backlash for Their Views

The realm of academia offers compelling examples of how individuals have been sidelined or ostracized for expressing views deemed unpalatable by some. The case of Bret Weinstein, a former biology professor at Evergreen State College, stands out. Weinstein faced severe backlash and was forced to resign after he raised concerns about a campus event that he believed was discriminatory. His attempt to engage in a dialogue about equity was met with aggressive protests and demands for his dismissal, highlighting the volatility of the academic environment when it comes to certain topics. Similarly, Jordan Peterson, a professor at the University of Toronto, stirred controversy for his opposition to certain Canadian compelled speech laws. Peterson's contention was that the legislation, though formulated to safeguard gender rights, inadvertently impinged on freedom of speech. His stance, while gaining many supporters, also led to vocal criticism, attempts to de-platform him, and sparked fierce debates in academic and public circles alike. These episodes illuminate that even in nations celebrated for their democratic principles and freedoms, expressing contrarian viewpoints can lead to unforeseen, and often disproportional, consequences.

## A Look into the Controversial Works that Sparked Outrage

Dissent, by its very nature, tends to shake the foundations of accepted norms, and in the world of art and literature, this often translates to controversial works that ignite fervent debates. For instance, the Danish cartoons of the Prophet Muhammad in 2005 led to global outrage, protests, and even deaths. It raised a pressing question: where does one draw the line between freedom of expression and respect for religious sentiments? Another illustrative instance is Salman Rushdie's "The Satanic Verses." This novel, perceived as blasphemous by some, resulted in death threats and a fatwa calling for Rushdie's assassination. Such controversies highlight the intricate dance between intention, interpretation, and public sentiment. They force society to confront the ever-evolving boundaries of what is deemed 'acceptable' and ponder whether political correctness, in its quest to protect, might often stifle the very voices it aims to amplify.

## *Platforms, Publishers, and Gatekeepers: Curators of Modern Discourse*

### The Intermediaries in the Communication Chain

In the age of information, while there exists an illusion of boundless freedom in speech and expression, certain entities possess a disproportionate influence over what gets communicated to the masses. These entities, comprising of social media platforms, publishing houses, and other media gatekeepers, act as intermediaries in the vast communication chain. Their role, while initially perceived as mere platforms or facilitators, has evolved—or devolved, depending on one's perspective—into that of arbiters of acceptable discourse. Platforms such as Twitter, Facebook, and YouTube, which boast billions of users globally, have algorithms and policies that can promote or bury content based on criteria often opaque to the general public. Similarly, publishing houses, film producers, and TV networks decide which voices get magnified and which are stifled. Their choices, often made under the guise of adhering to political correctness, can lead to an echo chamber, suppressing diversity of thought.

### Their Influence on What Gets Voiced and What Remains Hidden

Their Influence on What Gets Voiced and What Remains Hidden The influence of these intermediaries is not just vast but also deeply intertwined with governmental directives. With increasing frequency, governments are dictating to these platforms what is "acceptable" and what is not, branding divergent views as "misinformation" when they do not align with official stances or objectives. A subtle blend of corporate cautiousness and government intervention means that the scope of what is allowed in public discourse is increasingly narrowing. With just a simple tweak in an algorithm, platforms can promote content they or the governing bodies deem "safe", while burying what they consider "controversial".

This kind of control has ramifications. Voices that challenge dominant narratives, bring forth unconventional insights, or deviate from the politically correct trajectory find themselves overshadowed or silenced. For example, authors keen on exploring contentious issues or presenting non-mainstream perspectives may face obstacles in getting their works published. Their challenges aren't always rooted in the merit of their content but often arise from anticipated backlash rooted in PC or governmental guidelines. In contrast, creators conforming to the approved narrative receive disproportionate visibility, contributing to a monotonous and controlled public discourse.

The implications of this controlled discourse are profound. As society becomes conditioned to a sanitized version of discourse, it stands to miss out on transformative ideas, pioneering narratives, and avant-garde thought processes—all of which might be deemed too risky in the current climate. This interplay between corporations, governmental oversight, and self-censorship risks breeding a culture of conformity, where innovation and contrarian viewpoints are the casualties.

**Case Studies: When Gatekeepers Chose to Silence Rather than Amplify**

One notable example is the case of James Damore, a former Google engineer who penned a memo questioning the company's diversity policies. The memo, which aimed to present a different perspective on gender disparities in tech, quickly became a hotbed of controversy. Google's decision to fire Damore for his views was seen by many as a testament to the company's inability to tolerate dissenting opinions, particularly ones that stray from the accepted PC narrative. In the literary world, the controversy surrounding the novel "American Dirt" by Jeanine Cummins offers another case study. Despite its initial acclaim, the book faced backlash over its portrayal of Mexican migrants, leading to canceled book tours and public apologies. Many wondered if publishers would become even more risk-averse in the future, favoring works that adhered strictly to PC guidelines. These instances underline the profound influence gatekeepers have in shaping public discourse and the dangers of wielding this power without allowing space for diverse voices.

## *The Modern Noose: Subtle Strangulation in the Digital Age*

### Recognizing the New Forms of Suppression

In the past, suppression of speech was evident through actions such as book burnings, public ostracizations, or even arrests. Today, however, the methods of silencing dissenting voices have become more nuanced and discreet, yet equally effective, if not more so. This modern suppression often operates under the guise of adherence to community standards, platform policies, or the nebulous realm of "hate" speech definitions. For instance, a social media post may be shadow banned—a tactic where the content is not outright deleted, but its visibility is severely limited without the knowledge of the poster. Another form is "deplatforming," where individuals are removed from platforms entirely, cutting off their primary means of communication with their audience. These measures, while introduced as methods to foster respectful dialogue, can be weaponized as tools to suppress non-conforming opinions.

### The Role of Technology in Monitoring Speech

Technology, in many ways, has become the proverbial double-edged sword. On the one hand, it offers unparalleled avenues for free expression, enabling anyone with an internet connection to share their views. However, it also provides the means for unprecedented surveillance and control. Algorithms are capable of scanning vast amounts of data, flagging content that goes against predetermined criteria. Automated systems, devoid of human nuances, determine what's "appropriate" or "inappropriate" based on a set code, often leading to overzealous censorship. A classic example from the past would be the automatic demonetization or flagging of YouTube videos discussing sensitive topics, even when they were educational or news-related. This technological oversight, while designed to create safer online spaces, inadvertently promotes a culture of self-censorship, as users become wary of crossing unseen boundaries.

**The Emerging Challenges of Navigating a Digital-First World**

Navigating the digital landscape today is akin to walking through a minefield, where a single misstep can result in an explosion of public outrage, platform penalties, or both. As the digital realm becomes an integral part of daily life, the stakes rise significantly. A tweet from a decade ago can be unearthed and used to tarnish one's reputation today. Online mobs, often driven more by the thrill of the hunt than by genuine grievances, can launch coordinated attacks, leading to job losses, mental health issues, or even forcing individuals into hiding.

An illustrative case could be that of Justine Sacco, In December 2013, Justine, a relatively unknown PR executive, boarded a flight from London to South Africa. Before taking off, she sent out a tweet intended as a satirical comment on American ignorance about HIV/AIDS: "Going to Africa. Hope I don't get AIDS. Just kidding. I'm white!" By the time her flight landed 11 hours later, her life had irrevocably changed.

The tweet, which many saw as racially insensitive and dismissive of the AIDS epidemic in Africa, went viral. As it spread, public outrage grew exponentially. Twitter users, many of whom had never met or even heard of Sacco, branded her a racist, demanded her termination from her job, and even wished physical harm upon her. Before she could even comprehend the scale of the backlash, she became the number one global trend on Twitter. It was a digital public shaming on a scale few had seen up until that point.

To make matters worse, she was completely oblivious to the firestorm during her flight due to the absence of in-flight Wi-Fi. When she landed and turned on her phone, she was met with a barrage of hateful messages, notifications, and missed calls. The narrative had spiraled out of control, and the online mob had already passed judgment.

She lost her job. Her personal information, including her home address, was doxed. Friends and acquaintances distanced themselves. The single tweet had not only made her a pariah online but had real-world consequences that affected her professional and personal life.

The Justine Sacco episode is emblematic of the dangers lurking in the digital realm, especially in an era defined by rapid information dissemination and 'cancel culture'. It underscores the perilous nature of online interactions, where a single comment, joke, or observation can be taken out of context, misconstrued, or deliberately twisted. The online world, with its instant feedback loops and often decontextualized snippets of information, can amplify the worst of mob behaviors. In Sacco's case, a tweet intended as satire (though admittedly in poor taste) became a lightning rod for outrage, destroying her reputation and upending her life in mere hours. It serves as a stark reminder that, in the age of political correctness and instantaneous digital reactions, the border between one's online actions and real-world consequences has never been more porous.

## *Resistance and Resilience: The Undying Spirit of Expression*

### Celebrating Voices that Refuse to Be Hushed

Throughout history, attempts to suppress voices have been met with resistance from defiant souls who refuse to bow to the whims of authority or the majority. In the age of political correctness, this spirit remains undimmed. Some notable figures have stood tall amidst waves of criticism, not just defending their right to speak but also the essence of what they spoke. Take J.K. Rowling, for instance. The famed author faced backlash for her comments on gender and sex, but instead of receding into the shadows, she continued to articulate her views, championing the importance of open dialogue. Such figures, whether one agrees with them or not, represent the resilience of human spirit and the belief that truth, in all its complexities, must be discussed rather than buried.

## The Methods Employed to Bypass Traditional Gatekeeping

As the avenues of mainstream expression become increasingly narrow, innovators find alternative routes to make themselves heard. The internet, for all its pitfalls, offers a plethora of platforms for uncensored and unrestricted content. Podcasts have emerged as a particularly potent medium in this context. Figures like Joe Rogan, Jordan Peterson, and others have used this platform to discuss controversial topics, often inviting guests from diverse viewpoints. Similarly, platforms like Substack have enabled writers to share their thoughts directly with readers, bypassing traditional media gatekeeping. Crowdfunding campaigns, direct patronage, and decentralized platforms further empower creators to remain independent, ensuring their voice remains authentic, untamed, and unfiltered.

## Stories of Triumph Amidst Adversity

One stirring account of resilience in the face of overwhelming adversity is that of Sir Tim Hunt, a Nobel laureate. During a conference, he made remarks about the "trouble with girls" in scientific labs, which, taken out of context, resulted in a global outcry. Although he intended his comments as light-hearted, ironic remarks to support female scientists, they were misinterpreted. Facing immense backlash, he eventually resigned from his honorary positions. However, instead of fading into the shadows, Hunt continued to passionately contribute to the world of science, emphasizing the importance of open dialogue and understanding in academic settings. He remains an emblematic figure, illustrating both the potential dangers of misinterpretation in our hyper-connected age and the resilience of the human spirit. Stories like Hunt's serve as a beacon, reminding us of the challenges of navigating today's intricate socio-cultural milieu while underscoring the power of unwavering commitment to one's beliefs.

## *The Era of "Fact-Checkers":*
## *Bias and Influence from Powerhouses*

### Origins and Purpose

The advent of the internet brought with it an era of information overload. As the volume of online content proliferated, discerning factual information from falsehoods became a mounting challenge. To combat this, the concept of "fact-checking" was born. Initially, fact-checkers were hailed as the guardians of truth, their primary role being to verify claims and ensure the public had access to accurate information. They emerged as the solution to fake news, biased reporting, and deliberate disinformation.

### Concerns of Bias and Influence

However, as fact-checking institutions gained prominence, concerns began to arise. Many of these organizations are funded, either directly or indirectly, by powerful corporations, "philanthropists", or even government entities. This financial connection raises legitimate questions about impartiality. For instance, if a major tech company funds a fact-checking platform, would that platform be as rigorous in verifying claims that could harm the company's reputation or bottom line? Similarly, if a government supports a fact-checking body, to what extent might this body avoid contradicting official stances or narratives?

Furthermore, the criteria for what gets fact-checked and how determinations are made are not always transparent. While many fact-checkers claim to operate based on clear, objective standards, the reality is often murkier. Two different fact-checkers might rate the same claim differently based on their interpretations, methodologies, or even biases. This inconsistency poses a dilemma: If fact-checkers, who are supposed to be the bastions of truth, can't agree on what's factual, where does that leave the public?

**The Interplay with Big Corporations and Governments**

The relationship between fact-checkers, corporations, and governments is particularly concerning to many. As previously mentioned, funding can be a significant influence. But it's not just about money. In the era of cancel culture and political correctness, corporations and governments might leverage their influence over fact-checkers to suppress certain viewpoints or narratives. Labeling a piece of information as "misinformation" has become a powerful tool to silence dissenting voices, especially when these labels are endorsed by prominent fact-checking entities.

For example, in certain countries, fact-checkers have been accused of siding with government narratives, especially when it comes to politically sensitive topics. Instead of challenging or verifying government claims, these fact-checkers sometimes appear to act as amplifiers, reinforcing official viewpoints while dismissing or undermining alternative perspectives.

**Concluding Thoughts**

Today, "fact-checkers" have zero credibility, as they should. They have been proven to be corrupt and they themselves are the ones spreading misinformation. While fact-checking, in theory, is a commendable endeavor, its execution in today's complex web of interests poses significant challenges. For fact-checkers to genuinely serve the public good, there needs to be a commitment to transparency, impartiality, and independence from external pressures, whether they come from corporate boardrooms or government offices. Only then can the public trust that the "facts" presented to them are indeed unbiased truths, rather than curated narratives shaped by unseen hands.

## *Towards a More Open Discourse:*
## *Seeking Balance in the Age of Sensitivity*

### The Need for a Balanced Approach to Political Correctness

The essence of political correctness, stripped of its extremities, was always about fostering respect and ensuring that people were not marginalized based on race, gender, religion, or any other social markers. But like a pendulum that's swung too far in one direction, there's been an evident overreach. This overreach, as many argue, has come at the expense of free discourse, open debate, and even the pursuit of truth in certain contexts. Consider the academic world, where certain research topics are deemed too sensitive to be discussed openly, leading scholars to abandon or self-censor their work. For instance, there have been instances where examining biological differences between sexes, a valid scientific inquiry, has met fierce resistance. A balanced approach necessitates that while respect remains paramount, fear of misinterpretation should not halt academic pursuits.

### Finding the Middle Ground: Respecting Sensibilities without Stifling Voices

The key to a thriving society is an active marketplace of ideas where thoughts, regardless of their popularity, can be presented, debated, and either accepted or refuted based on their merits. For this to function, there must be a mutual respect between the speaker and the listener. The speaker should be aware of and considerate towards the cultural and personal backgrounds of their audience. At the same time, listeners must understand the context and intention behind words, rather than honing in on isolated phrases that might offend. A classic case in point is the uproar that often surrounds comedians who use satire and irony to discuss sensitive topics. While it's essential to call out genuinely harmful rhetoric, it's equally crucial to differentiate between malicious intent and comedic or literary exploration.

**The Way Forward: Building a More Inclusive yet Expressive Society**

As society grapples with the ridiculousness of political correctness, it's imperative to look towards a future where both respect and expression are given their due. This involves creating platforms where people feel safe to voice their opinions, even if they're unpopular, without the fear of undue backlash. Simultaneously, there must be an emphasis on education and open dialogue, helping individuals understand diverse perspectives and the reasons behind various sensitivities. Schools, universities, and public forums can play a pivotal role in this by encouraging debates, fostering critical thinking, and emphasizing the importance of context. By doing so, society can move towards an era where the idea of political correctness serves its intended purpose: not as a tool for suppression, but as a guideline for understanding and mutual respect.

# Chapter 3
# Cancel Culture and the Social Media Circus

### *The Digital Amplifier:*
### *Navigating the Boons and Banes of the Online World*

## How Platforms like Twitter and Facebook Magnify Cancel Culture's Effects

In the age of digital ubiquity, platforms like Twitter and Facebook serve as the modern agora, the central squares where individuals come together to discuss, debate, and disseminate ideas. Yet, the vast reach of these platforms has amplified the effects of cancel culture to unprecedented levels. While traditional media could generate outrage, the virality that social media platforms provide means that any given controversy can reach millions, even billions, within mere hours. A simple tweet can spiral into a global scandal, and a Facebook post can generate enough outrage to end careers.

## Analyzing the Speed and Ferocity of Online Backlashes

The digital age, marked by instant communication and the constant thirst for content, ensures that controversies flare up with astonishing speed. In this realm, there is little room for nuance or waiting for the complete story. Snap judgments, made by thousands, sometimes without full context, can lead to severe real-world consequences. Additionally, the anonymity provided by these platforms emboldens users, often unleashing a ferocity in backlashes that might not manifest in face-to-face interactions. This digital mob mentality is fueled by a sense of collective righteousness, where individual voices clamor to be part of a perceived larger justice movement. Yet, in the process, they often ignore the principle of "innocent until proven guilty."

A poignant example of this was the online furor surrounding the Covington Catholic High School students. The incident involving the Covington Catholic High School students serves as a compelling example of the challenges and risks associated with online backlashes. In this incident, a short video clip circulated on social media, showing a confrontation between a group of high school students, predominantly wearing "Make America Great Again" (MAGA) hats, and a Native American elder during a protest in Washington, D.C. The initial clip portrayed the students in a negative light, with some viewers interpreting their behavior as disrespectful and confrontational.

The video quickly went viral, sparking outrage and condemnation from many individuals and media outlets. It appeared to fit a particular narrative about political polarization and racial tension in the United States, and this narrative took hold within the digital sphere. As a result, the students faced a swift and intense online backlash, including threats of physical harm, doxxing (revealing personal information online), and widespread public shaming.

However, as more extended footage of the incident became available and additional context emerged, it became evident that the initial clip did not capture the full complexity of the situation. The extended footage revealed a more nuanced picture, showing that the encounter was more complicated than it had initially seemed. Some of the students claimed they were trying to defuse a tense situation rather than instigate it.

This incident highlights the dangers of forming snap judgments in the age of instant digital communication. The rush to judgment, fueled by the anonymity and rapid spread of information on social media platforms, can have severe real-world consequences. In the Covington Catholic High School case, the students faced threats to their safety and reputations before a full understanding of the situation emerged. It underscores the importance of seeking the complete story, practicing critical thinking, and adhering to the principle of "innocent until proven guilty" when engaging in online discourse, particularly when allegations are involved.

In retrospect, the incident serves as a cautionary tale about the impact of digital mob mentality and the need for more thoughtful and nuanced discussions in the online realm, even in the face of controversy.

## The Double-Edged Sword: The Power and Pitfalls of Global Communication

The democratization of communication, thanks to platforms like Twitter and Facebook, has undeniably brought power to the masses. Movements like #MeToo, which highlighted systemic sexual harassment, gained traction, and created tangible change primarily due to their virality on social media. However, this immense power also comes with pitfalls. The same platforms that amplify righteous causes can also magnify misunderstandings, half-truths, or even deliberate misinformation. Furthermore, the global nature of these platforms means that cultural nuances can get lost in translation, leading to unnecessary outrage. For instance, a gesture or phrase deemed innocuous in one culture might be deeply offensive in another, and without understanding this context, global audiences might inadvertently partake in or support cancel campaigns based on misunderstandings. The challenge, then, is to harness the power of these platforms while remaining vigilant against their potential for misrepresentation and undue harm.

## *The Casualties of Cancelation:*
## *Navigating the Storms of Online Outrage*

### Stories of Personal and Professional Destruction

The stories of those who've faced the wrath of cancel culture are varied, but a common thread is the disproportionate punishment meted out for mistakes. Many times, these individuals face consequences that far outweigh the severity of their actions. Take the case of James Gunn, director of the "Guardians of the Galaxy" movies. Tweets from a decade ago, which he had already apologized for and disavowed, resurfaced. Despite the context of those tweets being dark humor, and Gunn's evident personal growth since then, he was swiftly fired from directing the third movie in the series (though later rehired due to public and industry support). Similarly, professors have been ousted from academic positions, authors have had book deals canceled, and ordinary citizens have faced dire personal and professional setbacks all because of moments of indiscretion or misunderstood statements that went viral.

**Evaluating the Fairness of the Trials Held in the Court of Public Opinion**

The court of public opinion, facilitated by social media platforms, operates on a very different set of rules than traditional justice systems. Here, judgments are swift, juries are massive, and evidence is often based on snippets of information devoid of context. The question arises: is this system fair? Traditional justice systems, for all their flaws, are predicated on principles like "innocent until proven guilty" and proportionate punishment. In the realm of online cancel culture, however, these principles are often discarded. Instead, individuals are frequently presumed guilty, and the punishment meted out is often harsh and uncompromising. The inability of many online mobs to allow for redemption or growth reflects a lack of nuance, understanding, and intelligence. For instance, the case of Kevin Hart stepping down from hosting the Oscars due to past tweets raised questions about whether society allows individuals to evolve and grow from past mistakes, or if they're forever doomed to be judged by them. The real concern is the oversimplification of complex human behaviors and the disregard for the multifaceted nature of individual growth and redemption.

## *The Mobs and Their Torches:*
## *The Dark Underbelly of Online Outrage*

**Delving into the Psychology of the Online Cancel Crusader**

The rise of cancel culture has unmasked a fascinating, if somewhat unsettling, side of human behavior. When part of an online mob, individuals often display amplified emotions and reduced inhibitions. This is underpinned by the online disinhibition effect, where anonymity, invisibility, and a lack of immediate feedback can lead to more aggressive and less restrained behavior. For instance, the tragic case of Caroline Flack, a UK television presenter who took her own life following relentless online scrutiny and criticism, revealed the depths of cruelty that can be amplified in the echo chambers of social media. Some might argue that being part of a larger group provides a feeling of righteousness or validation, allowing participants to bypass self-reflection on their own actions. The guise of anonymity or sheer distance (being behind a screen) emboldens many to voice opinions they might never express face-to-face. They need to grasp the significance of their actions. If only there was a way for instant feedback, a figurative punch in the face. Then, and only then, would people start taking responsibility for their actions and start to understand.

## Identifying Patterns in Mob Behavior

If one were to observe the anatomy of online outrage, certain patterns become discernible. It often begins with a 'call-out,' where an individual or entity is highlighted for alleged wrongdoing. This is swiftly followed by virality as the issue is shared and reshared, amassing a larger audience. As more join in the outcry, the original message often becomes distorted, with the narrative focusing less on the initial issue and more on the collective indignation. Confirmation bias plays a significant role here. People seek information that aligns with their pre-existing beliefs and feelings, further entrenching their stance.

## Recognizing the Thin Line Between Justice Seeking and Vengefulness

While many online movements start with genuine intentions of seeking justice or raising awareness about problematic behavior, there's a precarious balance that can easily tip towards vengefulness. When the collective goal shifts from addressing the issue to punishing the individual, the movement becomes less about justice and more about revenge. The digital age has made it easy to conflate the two, especially when the emotional high of participating in a trending hashtag blurs the line between activism and aggression. One must ponder, for instance, when celebrities like Taylor Swift or James Charles have faced online backlashes, was the aim to make them aware of their perceived wrongs or to derive satisfaction from their downfall? The virality and speed of online discourse make it challenging to pause, reflect, and differentiate between a genuine call for accountability and the dangerous allure of a witch hunt.

### Distinguishing Justice from Vendetta: Navigating the Nuances of Online Outrage

**When is the Outrage Valid, and When is it a Product of Mob Mentality?**

The age-old adage, "Where there's smoke, there's fire," often rings true. Yet, in the digital age, smoke can be artificially produced and fire falsely claimed. Distinguishing genuine concerns from the din of an orchestrated outrage can be a complex task. Valid outrage usually stems from an incident or statement that inherently goes against widely accepted societal values or ethics. Such outrage often seeks resolution or an apology. On the other hand, outrage that emerges from mob mentality may not always have a well-defined cause. Instead, it feeds on emotions, amplifying them without seeking constructive resolution. A real-life illustration of this gray area was the #MeToo movement. While it served as a powerful platform for many genuine victims of harassment and abuse, there were also instances where accusations were made without substantial evidence, leading to heated debates about the movement's validity and intention.

**Case Studies Differentiating Genuine Accountability Calls from Targeted Attacks**

A quintessential example of a genuine call for accountability was the outrage following the Cambridge Analytica scandal, where Facebook was found to have mishandled user data, potentially influencing elections. The public's demand for transparency and better data protection protocols was rooted in valid concerns about privacy and the ethical use of data.

## The Responsibility of Bystanders in Shaping Narratives

The Internet has transformed passive audiences into active participants. As tweets are retweeted and posts are shared, bystanders play a pivotal role in shaping and amplifying narratives. This dynamic comes with its own set of responsibilities. First and foremost is the duty of due diligence. Before joining a digital mob or supporting a cause, verifying the authenticity of the information is crucial. Secondly, there's a responsibility to maintain a sense of proportion in responses. Amplifying a narrative doesn't always mean escalating it. Finally, there's the responsibility of introspection: assessing one's motivations for supporting a particular narrative. Are they championing a cause for justice, or is it the seductive allure of being part of a larger, dominating group?

An example that encapsulates the power of bystanders was the incident involving the young "Star Wars" actress Kelly Marie Tran. Kelly Marie Tran's casting as Rose Tico in the Star Wars sequel trilogy was groundbreaking. As the first woman of color to play a lead role in the iconic saga, her presence was a win for representation and diversity. However, not all were pleased. From the moment her character graced the big screen in "Star Wars: The Last Jedi", Tran became the target of relentless online harassment. Critics attacked her on grounds of her race, gender, and character's significance in the film. These critiques quickly devolved into personal attacks, leading Tran to face a barrage of hateful messages every day.

The intensity and virulence of these attacks were shocking. Some questioned the very essence of her identity, while others made derogatory remarks about her appearance. Such sustained, aggressive online behavior took its toll. Less than a year after the movie's release, Tran decided to delete all her Instagram posts, effectively removing her voice from a platform where she once joyfully engaged with fans. In a later op-ed for The New York Times, she described the deep emotional impact of the harassment, revealing how it led her to question her self-worth and place in society.

However, the narrative didn't end with Tran's retreat. As news of her departure from social media spread, there was an outpouring of support from fans, colleagues, and even strangers. Fellow actors, directors, and prominent figures within the entertainment industry rallied around Tran, condemning the toxic elements within the fanbase and championing the importance of representation. The hashtag #FanArtforRose emerged, where artists from around the world shared positive illustrations of her character. This countermovement showcased the Internet's ability to heal as much as it harms. It demonstrated that bystanders, when mobilized, have the power to drown out hate with messages of love and acceptance.

In this context, the Kelly Marie Tran incident serves as both a warning and an inspiration. It's a stark reminder of how quickly online platforms can become breeding grounds for hate and prejudice. Yet, it also highlights the immense power of collective action, where bystanders can transition from passive observers to active defenders, turning the tide against toxicity and championing the values of empathy and inclusivity.

## *Creating a Healthier Digital Society:*
## *Navigating the Narrow Straits of Online Interactions*

### Addressing the Toxic Elements of Online Interactions

The internet, with its vast expanse and the promise of anonymity, has become a breeding ground for toxicity. The very structure of certain platforms encourages polarization. Features like 'likes', 'retweets', or 'upvotes' mean that extreme views often get amplified, while nuanced discussions get buried. The ephemeral nature of online interactions, where people can 'tweet and forget,' also means that users sometimes don't face immediate consequences for their aggressive or impulsive remarks. Add to this the problem of echo chambers, where algorithms feed users' content similar to what they've liked or engaged with before, and you have a digital realm where biases are reinforced, and different perspectives are rarely encountered. For instance, during political events, social media can become a battleground where differing opinions aren't debated but vilified, leading to a fragmented and antagonistic digital society.

## Advocating for Patience, Research, and Empathy

The antidote to impulsiveness and aggressive cancelation attempts lies in cultivating patience, emphasizing research, and fostering empathy. For every viral tweet or post that demands immediate reaction, there's value in taking a moment to understand context and ascertain facts. In a world of fake news and misinformation, research is more critical than ever. Blindly sharing or endorsing information without verifying its authenticity can lead to harmful consequences. But beyond patience and research, the most crucial element is empathy. Digital interactions often lack the humanizing element of face-to-face conversations. Behind every screen is a person with feelings, fears, and aspirations. Monica Lewinsky's TED talk, "The Price of Shame," highlights this beautifully, urging individuals to see the human behind the headlines. By practicing empathy online, society can move towards a more understanding and less aggressive digital landscape.

## Crafting a Digital World that Values Justice Without Compromising on Compassion

In the quest for justice, the digital realm sometimes overshoots, turning into a space of relentless persecution. While accountability is crucial, there's a need to strike a balance so that the digital world doesn't become a dystopian space where every mistake is met with irreversible consequences. To achieve this, platform creators and users alike must prioritize creating spaces that encourage understanding and rehabilitation over blind punishment. This includes building algorithms that prioritize diverse views, fostering online communities that value growth, and encouraging online etiquette education. One such initiative is the rise of "restorative justice" online forums where individuals discuss transgressions, understand the harm caused, and work towards collective healing. If platforms can prioritize these values and users champion them, the digital realm can transform into a space that is just but also compassionate, echoing the better angels of our nature.

# Chapter 4
# Division in the Name of Inclusion

*Identity Politics and Fragmentation:*
*When Unity is Undermined by Segregation*

**How Representation Goals Sometimes Inadvertently Lead to Pigeonholing**

While the core ethos of identity politics is commendable, in recent times, the quest for representation has often morphed into an excessive focus on labels. The push for inclusivity sometimes runs the risk of becoming so granular that individuals feel pressured to define themselves by a myriad of intersecting identity markers. For instance, instead of simply identifying as a member of the LGBTQ+ community, there might be pressure to specify one's identity further, leading to terms like "pansexual, non-binary, Latinx individual." While it's essential for people to find their personal identity and represent it, this hyper-focus can inadvertently lead to pigeonholing, where people are boxed into increasingly narrow categories. This can create a situation where the broader message of unity and common cause becomes obscured by an overwhelming array of micro-identities that are simply ridiculous and serve no other purpose than giving the individual a false sense of importance.

**The Dangerous Dance of Categorization and Its Societal Implications**

Categorizing individuals, even with the best of intentions, can be a double-edged sword. On the one hand, it allows marginalized groups to rally together, find common ground, and advocate for their rights. On the other, excessive categorization will foster an "us versus them" mentality. When identity politics becomes too factionalized, it will inadvertently fuel division and infighting within movements. For example, debates about "who has it worse" in terms of oppression will create rifts within communities that should be working together. Furthermore, there's a risk that individuals who don't neatly fit into any category or who straddle multiple categories might feel alienated or excluded. The societal implication is a landscape where the conversation shifts from broader issues of justice and equality to disputes over labels and categories. Instead of fostering unity and common purpose, the very tool that was meant to empower will become a source of division.

## *Echo Chambers of Division:*
## *When Digital Walls Segregate Us Further*

### The Nature and Nurture of Online Bubbles

At its inception, the internet was hailed as the ultimate democratizer, a space where voices from all over the globe could congregate, share, and discuss in an open forum. Yet, as the years have gone by and as digital platforms have evolved, we've noticed a peculiar and somewhat paradoxical trend: rather than expanding our horizons, the internet often narrows them. Enter the phenomenon of online bubbles, or echo chambers. These are digital spaces where users are repeatedly exposed to information that conforms to their pre-existing beliefs, effectively shielding them from diverse viewpoints. The nature of these bubbles stems from human psychology: we're inherently inclined to seek validation and shy away from cognitive dissonance. Online platforms, in their quest to deliver personalized user experiences, nurture these tendencies, thereby creating environments that amplify our biases instead of challenging them.

### How Algorithms Reinforce and Deepen Divisions

Algorithms, especially those employed by social media giants like Facebook, Twitter, and YouTube, play a central role in creating and maintaining these echo chambers. Driven by data and designed to maximize user engagement, these algorithms often prioritize content that aligns with a user's established preferences. For instance, if a user frequently interacts with conservative political content, the algorithm is more likely to suggest similar conservative channels, pages, or posts, further entrenching the user's worldview. This feedback loop, where content consumption informs recommendations, which in turn dictates further consumption, deepens divisions. Users end up in a self-reinforcing cycle, often unaware that their online reality is but a fraction of the broader narrative. It's a system that values user retention over holistic information exposure, inadvertently promoting polarization.

**Real-world Repercussions of Living in a Virtual Echo Chamber**

Living within these digital cocoons has tangible effects on our real-world perceptions and interactions. Firstly, continual exposure to one-sided information can lead to an overestimation of the prevalence and popularity of one's beliefs—a phenomenon known as the "false consensus effect." This can result in surprise, frustration, and even disbelief when confronted with differing opinions in the real world, as was evident in the shock of many during political events like the Brexit vote or the 2016 US Presidential election. Furthermore, when one's beliefs are rarely challenged, they can become more extreme over time. Without counterarguments or alternative perspectives, there's little to moderate one's views. This has real-world implications, from strained personal relationships to an increasingly polarized political climate where compromise becomes elusive. A striking example is the proliferation of propaganda, where individuals, deeply ensconced in their echo chambers, become impervious to real facts and mainstream narratives, often leading to misinformed actions and trust in established institutions. These people disbelieve anything contradictory and label everything as conspiracy theories.

## *The Irony of Exclusion: When the Quest for Inclusivity Divides*

### Celebrating Diversity, But at What Cost?

Embracing diversity is a noble ideal. As societies around the world become more multicultural, the need for understanding and celebrating diverse perspectives becomes paramount. Yet, in some circles, the celebration of diversity has taken on an almost competitive edge. The aspiration to showcase myriad voices occasionally morphs into a contest of who can be the most diverse or the most inclusive, occasionally eclipsing the true purpose of understanding and empathy. This "competitive inclusivity" can sometimes result in superficial gestures that lack depth or genuine appreciation. For instance, a brand might include people of various backgrounds in its advertisement for the sake of appearing diverse, but not take meaningful steps to ensure diversity within its corporate structure. The intention behind the celebration becomes important; is it genuine appreciation or merely a performative act?

### Instances Where the Pursuit of Inclusivity Paradoxically Isolated Groups

While the aim of inclusivity is to foster understanding and unity, there are instances where it has had the opposite effect. One example that garnered significant media attention was the debate surrounding "safe spaces" on university campuses. While the original intention behind safe spaces was to provide marginalized groups a haven from potential prejudice or bigotry, in certain situations, these spaces were seen as exclusive clubs that barred individuals not belonging to a particular group. Critics argue that such practices, while rooted in good intentions, end up creating more division by segregating individuals based on identity markers. Another controversial instance arose when some events focused on biological women's issues did not resonate with all women, leading to debates about the inclusivity of such events. While the objective behind these events was to spotlight certain concerns, they inadvertently ended up sidelining some women who felt their experiences were not represented. These situations highlight the challenges and complexities of inclusivity and how even well-meaning actions can sometimes result in further divisions.

**Evaluating the Balance Between Representation and Unity**

The balance between representation and unity is a delicate one. On the one hand, every group, regardless of its size or influence, deserves to have its voice heard and its experiences acknowledged. On the other hand, an overemphasis on distinguishing every group can lead to a fragmented society where shared values and experiences are overshadowed by differences. So, where does one draw the line? It's crucial to remember that diversity isn't just about showcasing different identities; it's about interweaving these identities into a cohesive, shared narrative. True inclusivity fosters a sense of belonging for everyone, without anyone feeling sidelined or pigeonholed. A society's strength isn't just in its various voices, but in the harmonious chorus they can create together. To achieve this, the focus should shift from mere representation to genuine integration, where diverse groups don't just coexist but truly understand and empathize with one another.

## *Polarization and Public Discourse: From Civil Exchange to Bitter Divide*

**The Shift from Civil Debates to Hostile Divisions**

Historically, public discourse was perceived as a means for individuals to exchange ideas, challenge beliefs, and engage in constructive debates. These platforms, whether they be town halls or intellectual salons, were spaces for knowledge sharing and consensus building. However, in recent years, there has been a palpable shift. The tone of discussions, especially on contentious topics, has turned increasingly combative. People often enter these conversations not with the intent to understand or learn, but to defend their stance at all costs. The media, with its sensationalist tendencies, has sometimes further exacerbated this by highlighting the most extreme voices, overshadowing moderate perspectives. Take, for instance, the televised debates where participants often talk over each other, hurling accusations instead of crafting reasoned arguments. This environment isn't conducive to mutual respect or understanding, but rather fosters animosity and division.

## How Political Correctness Intensifies Ideological Battles

Political correctness, in its original intent, was about promoting respect and understanding, ensuring that language and actions did not marginalize or offend. However, its misapplication or extreme enforcement can sometimes act as fuel to the fire of ideological battles. When individuals fear being labeled as "incorrect" or "offensive", it stifles open dialogue. This is especially true in academic settings, where open discourse and challenging established norms are essential. For instance, professors and students alike have raised concerns about the consequences of discussing controversial topics or presenting unpopular viewpoints, fearing backlash or accusations of insensitivity. As a result, individuals often retreat to their respective ideological corners, only engaging with those who share their beliefs. This echo chamber effect further entrenches beliefs and heightens animosity towards those "on the other side".

## The Danger of a Society Where Middle Ground Seems Lost

The erosion of the middle ground is one of the most profound dangers of the current state of public discourse. When compromise and mutual respect are lost, society becomes a battleground of extremes. Policies, instead of being collaborative efforts, swing wildly with changing administrations or popular sentiment, causing instability and uncertainty. An example of this can be seen in certain policy decisions related to climate change or public health, where science and facts become secondary to ideological beliefs or political affiliations. Furthermore, when people can't find common ground, it affects the very social fabric, leading to estrangement among communities, friends, and even families.

A society that values only extremes loses its ability to innovate, adapt, and progress, as it becomes mired in constant battles without any clear direction or shared vision for the future.

## *The PC Language Labyrinth:*
## *A Complicated Pathway to Polite Conversation*

### Navigating the Intricate Maze of Acceptable Terms and Phrases

The advent of political correctness brought with it a complex lexicon of acceptable terms, designed to reflect the evolving understanding of identity, race, gender, and a myriad of other societal facets. While the intent behind this evolution is rooted in respect and recognition, the swift pace at which these changes occur often leaves many feeling overwhelmed. Everyday language, which was once considered neutral or benign, can suddenly be deemed problematic or offensive. For older generations, particularly, this navigation can feel like walking through a linguistic minefield, unsure when or where they might unintentionally "offend". For instance, the silly transition from "secretary" to "administrative assistant" or from "fireman" to "firefighter" seeks to remove gender biases, but the rapidity and scope of such changes can be challenging for many to keep up with.

### Stories of Misunderstandings, Genuine Mistakes, and Their Repercussions

Everyone, at some point, has made a linguistic "faux pas", but in the age of political correctness, these errors can carry significant weight. There's the story of a respected college professor who was reprimanded for using a term in class that was once academically accepted but had recently become contentious. Despite his genuine apology and acknowledgment of the oversight, the incident became a blemish on his decades-long career. In another instance, a celebrity's old tweets, which contained now-outdated terms, were dug up, leading to a massive online backlash and the loss of endorsements. Such stories highlight the relentless scrutiny individuals face and the unforgiving nature of public judgment, where genuine "mistakes", even those from the distant past, aren't easily forgiven even though there is nothing to forgive..

**The Evolving Lexicon of Political Correctness and Its Societal Impact**

The constantly shifting landscape of politically correct language, while rooted in noble intentions, has profound societal implications. On one hand, it pushes society towards a more inclusive and respectful dialogue, acknowledging the complexities of modern identities. On the other hand, it can create divisions, where those not "in the know" feel excluded or vilified for their linguistic missteps. Moreover, the focus on language, while important, sometimes overshadows the more pressing systemic issues at hand. For instance, while it's crucial to address someone by their correct pronouns, it's equally vital to address the systemic discriminations that transgender individuals face. By placing excessive emphasis on language alone, there's a risk of creating a society that's superficially correct but lacks depth in its pursuit of genuine inclusivity and understanding.

## Divided We Fall: The Perils of a Fragmented Society

**Analyzing the Long-Term Effects of a Splintered Society**

When societies splinter based on ideologies, identities, or any distinguishing factor, it's not just a momentary division; the long-term effects can be profound and far-reaching. Historically, civilizations that have been internally divided have faced not only socio-political challenges but also eventual decline or even collapse. One need not look far to see examples, such as the Roman Empire, whose internal divisions played a part in its downfall. In the context of political correctness, the rifts created between groups can lead to mutual mistrust, a lack of shared national identity, and a diminishing sense of community. While the initial aim of PC culture is to be inclusive, the inadvertent result can be a society where groups become increasingly insular, leading to a fractured nation that struggles to find common ground or shared purpose.

## The Dangers of Isolated Communities Without Intercommunication

Communities that become isolated from one another not only miss out on the rich tapestry of diverse perspectives but also run the risk of becoming echo chambers. Within such silos, ideas aren't challenged, biases aren't confronted, and narratives go unexamined. Over time, this lack of intercommunication can lead to radicalization or extremism. A real-world example can be seen in certain social media groups or forums that cater to a specific ideology. Within these circles, opposing views are often ridiculed or excluded, leading to a distorted sense of reality. The dangers here are twofold: firstly, individuals within these communities may develop a skewed view of the world, and secondly, these isolated groups can become breeding grounds for extremist views or actions. When communities do not engage in dialogue with one another, misconceptions proliferate, further widening the chasm between them.

## The Quest for a Unifying Narrative Amidst Increasing Fragmentation

As society becomes more segmented, the quest for a unifying narrative becomes paramount. Such a narrative serves as the glue holding disparate groups together, ensuring a shared vision and mutual understanding. Historically, nations have rallied around causes, ideals, or even external threats to foster unity. In today's politically correct climate, the challenge lies in creating a narrative that acknowledges and celebrates diversity while also emphasizing shared values and goals. One can argue that while recognizing individual identities and histories is vital, it's equally crucial to highlight the shared human experiences that bind us all. Without such a unifying thread, society risks descending into a collection of isolated communities, each suspicious of the other, and lacking the cohesion necessary for collective progress.

# *Reimagining Inclusivity: Beyond Divisive Representation*

## Envisioning a World Where Representation Doesn't Result in Division

In an ideal world, representation should enrich society by weaving diverse narratives into its fabric without causing division. However, as we've observed, the current trajectory of political correctness sometimes results in segmented, and often competitive, identity groups. In such a setting, representation can, paradoxically, become a source of division rather than unity. For instance, the 2016 Academy Awards faced criticism over the hashtag #OscarsSoWhite. While it pushed the industry towards more inclusivity, it also inadvertently gave rise to debates about whether subsequent nominations of people of color were deserved or just appeasements. This inadvertently leads to doubts over genuine talent and worthiness. Ideally, the emphasis should be on ensuring every voice, irrespective of its background, gets a fair chance to be heard without the accompanying baggage of doubt or skepticism.

## Strategies to Foster Genuine Unity in Diversity

One of the foundational strategies to promote unity in diversity is to shift the focus from group identities to individual narratives. By celebrating individual achievements and stories, we move away from broad-brush generalizations that can pigeonhole groups. Education plays a pivotal role in this. Curriculums should emphasize shared human experiences and values while also addressing the unique experiences of diverse groups. Next, creating platforms for inter-group dialogues can dispel myths and break down barriers. An example is the "Living Library" concept where individuals from various backgrounds "loan" themselves out as "books" for others to "read" through conversations. Such initiatives humanize abstract group labels, leading to genuine understanding. Lastly, encouraging collaboration among diverse groups for a common goal, like community projects or joint art exhibitions, can underscore the idea that unity and diversity aren't mutually exclusive.

## Moving from Mere Tokenism to True Inclusivity

Tokenism, or the practice of making symbolic gestures towards inclusion without genuine commitment, can be more harmful than outright exclusion. It reduces individuals to mere symbols, undermining their worth and contributions. For example, if a company hires a person of a certain ethnicity or gender simply to "tick a box" without creating an environment where they can genuinely thrive and contribute, it perpetuates stereotypes and hampers genuine inclusivity. True inclusivity goes beyond mere representation; it's about ensuring equitable opportunities and respect for all. This requires systematic changes: from companies auditing their hiring processes for biases to television and film industries ensuring that diverse characters have depth and agency in their narratives. In essence, moving from tokenism to true inclusivity is about authenticity, where every individual, regardless of their background, feels seen, heard, and valued for who they truly are.

# Chapter 5
# The Education System's PC Overhaul

## *Erasing Histories: A Revisionist Approach in Education*

### A Dive into Instances Where History Was Revised for Sensitivity

The quest to ensure sensitivity in the curriculum has led some educational institutions to revise, or sometimes outright omit, certain historical events or figures. One such controversial example is the debate surrounding Confederate monuments and namesakes in American schools. Advocates argue that these symbols represent a painful history of racial discrimination and should therefore be removed. Detractors, on the other hand, see them as crucial reminders of the nation's past, no matter how unpleasant. Similarly, certain European schools have faced scrutiny for glossing over the darker aspects of their colonial pasts in favor of more benign narratives. The motivation behind such revisions often stems from a well-intentioned place—a desire to create inclusive environments that don't inadvertently glorify oppression or violence.

### The Dilemma of Presenting Unfiltered Truth versus Avoiding Potential Hurt

At the heart of the debate is a genuine quandary: How does one teach the unvarnished truth about history without causing distress or perpetuating harmful stereotypes? Take, for example, the teaching of World War II. The horrors of the Holocaust are undeniable and integral to understanding the broader context of the war. However, care must be taken to ensure that such teachings don't unintentionally stigmatize German students or perpetuate anti-German sentiments. Another example can be found in the portrayal of Native Americans in U.S. textbooks. For decades, many of these texts either overlooked the atrocities committed against Native populations or depicted them in broad, stereotypical ways. While there's a pressing need to correct these misrepresentations, there's also a challenge in ensuring the corrected narrative doesn't paint settlers in an unduly negative light, fostering a sense of collective guilt.

**Long-Term Implications of a Generation Unaware of Unaltered History**

By sanitizing or modifying historical content, we risk raising a generation that is unaware of the complexities and nuances of the past. Such a generation might be ill-equipped to critically engage with the world's present challenges, given that many of these challenges have deep historical roots. Moreover, a diluted understanding of history can lead to the repetition of past mistakes, as the famous adage "those who cannot remember the past are condemned to repeat it" suggests. For instance, understanding the intricate socio-political factors leading to the rise of totalitarian regimes in the 20th century is crucial to prevent similar rises in the future. If these narratives are oversimplified or altered, students might lack the depth of understanding required to navigate contemporary political landscapes. Furthermore, an unaltered comprehension of history fosters empathy, resilience, and a sense of global citizenship. Without these, society might find itself more polarized, with groups clinging to fragmented, biased versions of the past.

## *Classroom Chaos:*
## *Navigating the Waters of Political Correctness in Education*

### The Classroom as a Battleground for Political Correctness

In recent years, the classroom has transformed from a space of learning to a contested battleground of political correctness. The emphasis on ensuring that all students feel represented, respected, and heard is indeed a commendable aim. Yet, the intensity of this focus can sometimes overshadow the primary goal of education: imparting knowledge. Discussions that once revolved around historical facts, literary critiques, or scientific phenomena now run the risk of being derailed by concerns over potentially offensive content. For instance, classic literature, once revered for its timeless exploration of human nature, is now dissected for elements deemed inappropriate by today's standards. While the aim is to create a more inclusive environment, this scrutiny sometimes stifles open discussion and impedes a comprehensive understanding of the subject matter.

## Notable Controversies and the Debates They Sparked

There have been numerous controversies where curriculums and classroom discussions were deemed "too offensive" or not politically correct enough. One particularly striking example was the movement to ban Mark Twain's "Adventures of Huckleberry Finn" from school libraries and reading lists. The novel, which openly discusses racism and uses period-appropriate language, was seen by some as perpetuating racial stereotypes. Detractors argued that the context in which the novel was written and its anti-racist themes were being overlooked in favor of a surface-level reading. Another controversy surrounds discussions of gender and sexuality in schools. In various districts across the U.S., debates have raged about how, when, and even if topics like sexual orientation or gender identity should be introduced. Proponents argue that these discussions promote understanding and inclusivity, while opponents believe they might be too mature or contrary to their personal beliefs.

## How Educators are Navigating this Sensitive Landscape and How Many Just Gave into It

Many educators, already burdened with the challenges of teaching, now find themselves walking a tightrope of political correctness. While some have tried to adapt by being more inclusive and thoughtful in their teaching methods, others feel stifled, fearing backlash for potential missteps. Some teachers opt for pre-approved scripts, avoiding any deviations that might lead to controversy. This can result in a sanitized version of the subject matter that lacks depth and nuance.

On the other hand, there are educators who, feeling overwhelmed by the constant scrutiny and potential pitfalls of the PC culture, have simply capitulated. Instead of challenging students with thought-provoking discussions, these educators might default to the most benign version of the curriculum, even if it means omitting crucial information. This approach, driven by a mix of fear and frustration, unfortunately deprives students of a holistic education. While the intention of creating a safer environment is noble, the end result can be an educational experience that's limited in scope and depth.

## *The Cost of Miseducation: The Underbelly of a PC-centric Education System*

### Beyond Textbooks: The Wider Implications of a PC-centric Education

An education system, at its heart, should aim to equip students with a comprehensive understanding of the world, honing their analytical and critical thinking skills. But as political correctness seeps into the very fabric of our educational institutions, we risk compromising on these objectives. The shift from a content-rich curriculum to a PC-centric one has implications that go well beyond textbooks. For instance, discussions that once thrived on debate, challenging perspectives, and exploring multifaceted aspects of an issue now often revolve around ensuring no one is offended. This type of environment may deter students from voicing alternative viewpoints or questioning widely accepted narratives for fear of backlash. Over time, this can stifle intellectual curiosity and discourage the pursuit of truth.

### Exploring Potential Knowledge Gaps and Misconceptions Among Students

The emphasis on sanitizing educational content to align with political correctness can lead to glaring knowledge gaps. When certain events, figures, or themes are deliberately omitted from curricula to avoid potential offense, students miss out on understanding them in their full complexity. For example, in the pursuit of presenting a more inclusive view of history, there might be an inclination to downplay or even omit less savory aspects of a revered leader's life. While the intention is to prevent perpetuating negative stereotypes, the result can be a skewed, one-dimensional understanding. Moreover, when subjects like science and biology are pressured to conform to PC standards, it can lead to misconceptions. If, for example, discussions about genetic differences between sexes are suppressed due to concerns about perpetuating gender stereotypes, students miss out on understanding fundamental biological concepts.

## The Societal Risks of an Uninformed or Misinformed Generation

A society's future hinges on its youth. When that youth is either uninformed or misinformed due to an education system overly preoccupied with political correctness, the long-term ramifications can be dire. For one, a generation that hasn't been taught to critically evaluate information can become easy prey to misinformation and propaganda. In an era dominated by social media and rapid information exchange, the ability to discern fact from fiction is more crucial than ever. Additionally, without a well-rounded understanding of history, including its blemishes, society risks repeating past mistakes. On a broader scale, an education system that prioritizes avoiding offense above all else might produce individuals less equipped to handle disagreements, leading to a society that's more polarized, less tolerant of differing viewpoints, and more inclined toward echo chambers. The irony is palpable: in trying to build a more inclusive society, we risk creating one that's more fragmented than ever.

## *Universities and the PC Influence:*
## *The Epicenter of Debate and Discord*

**Documenting the Rise of Political Correctness in Higher Education**

In recent years, universities, once revered as bastions of free thought and rigorous debate, have increasingly become epicenters of political correctness. Historically, higher education was designed to challenge prevailing notions, expand horizons, and expose students to a myriad of perspectives. However, over the decades, there's been a noticeable shift. Trigger warnings, safe spaces, and disinvitations of controversial speakers have become commonplace. In some instances, courses or reading lists have been modified to avoid potential triggers. While the intention behind these changes—providing a safe and inclusive environment for all students—is noble, there is growing concern that universities are erring on the side of overprotection. Yale's 2015 controversy, for example, where a faculty member's email about Halloween costumes led to a campus-wide furor, showcased how seemingly innocuous matters could ignite intense PC debates in university settings.

## How This Shift Impacts Disciplines Like Journalism and Entertainment

Political correctness in universities has rippled into various disciplines, perhaps most notably in journalism and entertainment. Journalism schools emphasize the importance of neutrality and objectivity. However, with the PC culture taking root, there's been a noticeable shift towards a certain kind of 'activist journalism'. Many young journalists now believe their primary duty isn't just to report the facts but to drive social change, often aligning with PC principles. While this isn't inherently negative, it poses the risk of sidelining objectivity. In entertainment studies, there's an increasing focus on representation, diversity, and avoiding stereotypes. While these are essential goals, some argue that it has led to a kind of self-censorship among budding artists and creators, fearing backlash for any content that might be deemed non-PC. Classic works of literature and art, sometimes embodying values of their times, are being reevaluated through the lens of modern political correctness, which can limit students' exposure to a diverse range of historical viewpoints.

**Weighing Academic Freedom Against the Desire to Avoid Causing Offense**

The crux of the matter lies in balancing academic freedom with the genuine desire to avoid causing harm or offense. Historically, universities have been places where ideas, no matter how unpopular, could be aired, debated, and dissected. This freedom was deemed essential for intellectual growth. However, in the modern PC climate, many educators feel they're walking on eggshells. Courses on controversial subjects, like religious studies or history, are particularly fraught. Professors may shy away from discussing certain topics or presenting certain viewpoints, fearing backlash from both students and administration. For instance, Harvard Law Professor Jeannie Suk Gersen highlighted the chilling effect on legal education, noting that discussing laws about sexual assault became a minefield. The dilemma is real and profound: how do institutions ensure that every student feels safe and respected without compromising the integrity of education and stifling academic freedom?

## *The Safe Space Paradox: Safety or Stifling?*

**Understanding the Motivations Behind Creating "Safe Spaces" And Why They May Not Be Emotionally Healthy**

Safe spaces, originally rooted in the women's and LGBTQ+ movements of the 1960s and 1970s, aimed to provide a haven for individuals marginalized by society. In the university context, they are designated areas where students can seek refuge from distressing or controversial ideas. The underlying sentiment is commendable: to create an environment where all students, particularly those from vulnerable backgrounds, can feel valued, respected, and safe. However, there's a flip side to this coin. Over-reliance on such spaces may discourage young adults from facing challenging, uncomfortable ideas, potentially hindering their emotional growth. Encountering and grappling with opposing perspectives is an integral part of personal and intellectual maturation. By insulating students from these experiences, universities might unintentionally be setting them up for greater emotional fragility in the real world, where such protective buffers often don't exist.

## Debating the Ridiculousness and Drawbacks of Trigger Warnings and Related Practices

Trigger warnings originated from the need to alert trauma survivors about content that could evoke painful memories, a genuine and valid concern. However, their application has grown increasingly broad in academic settings. Some educators feel compelled to place trigger warnings on classic literary works or historical texts, fearing potential backlash for not being sensitive enough. Shakespeare's "Titus Andronicus" or Ovid's "Metamorphoses," for instance, might be flagged for violent or sexually explicit content. While it's vital to support trauma survivors, over-application of trigger warnings can verge on the absurd. Furthermore, it might encourage avoidance rather than healing. Psychologically, exposure therapy, where individuals confront and process traumatic stimuli in safe, controlled environments, has been an effective treatment for PTSD. If universities overly rely on trigger warnings, they could unintentionally inhibit students from facing and processing their traumas, depriving them of potential healing moments.

## Considering the Possible Sheltering Effect and Its Consequences on Student Resilience

The larger concern with practices like safe spaces and trigger warnings is the potential sheltering effect on students. In real-world scenarios, one does not always have the luxury of a trigger warning before encountering distressing news, nor a safe space to retreat to after a challenging confrontation. Building resilience — the ability to recover from setbacks, adapt to change, and keep going in the face of adversity — is a critical life skill. By continually shielding students from discomfort, are universities inadvertently making them more vulnerable? A 2018 study published in the "Journal of Behavior Therapy and Experimental Psychiatry" suggested that trigger warnings might inadvertently confirm that certain topics are traumatic, potentially increasing anxiety in those exposed. In essence, while the intent behind these protective measures is laudable, they may, paradoxically, be doing more harm than good by potentially impeding the development of resilience and emotional toughness that students will undoubtedly need outside of campus walls.

## *Educating for the Real World: Are We Doing Enough?*

### The Challenge of Preparing Students for Diverse Opinions Outside Academia

Upon graduating, students will inevitably find themselves in a world teeming with diverse opinions, many of which might contradict their own beliefs or challenge their sensibilities. The protective bubble of academia, where the majority of viewpoints might align or where disagreements are handled with kid gloves, is not an accurate reflection of the real world. For instance, in 2017, a controversial speaker's planned appearance at UC Berkeley led to significant protests and eventual cancellation. Such instances raise concerns about how prepared students are to face dissenting opinions once they step outside university confines. By not exposing students to a full spectrum of ideas, including controversial ones, educational institutions might unintentionally be creating graduates ill-equipped to engage in productive discourse in more unregulated environments.

### The Role of Universities in Fostering Critical Thinking versus Protective Insulation

Traditionally, universities have been the bastions of free thought, critical thinking, and rigorous debate. They were places where ideas, no matter how radical or contrary, were dissected, debated, and either refuted or accepted based on their merits. However, with the rise of political correctness, there's a perceptible shift. The emphasis now seems to lean more towards insulating students from potential harm or offense, sometimes at the cost of rigorous intellectual debate. Take, for instance, the disinvitation of speakers holding contentious views or the reluctance to discuss certain topics in classrooms for fear of offending. While protection of students from harm is paramount, it's worth questioning if this approach is at the expense of fostering robust critical thinking skills.

**Strategies for Bridging the Gap Between Academia and Societal Realities**

To truly prepare students for the real world, there's a pressing need to bridge the widening chasm between academia and societal realities. Firstly, universities could proactively facilitate debates and discussions that encompass a full range of viewpoints, ensuring students engage with, rather than avoid, challenging ideas. By doing so, they'd be fostering an environment of intellectual resilience. Secondly, there's a case for experiential learning — internships, field projects, and other real-world engagements that force students out of their comfort zones and into the practicalities of everyday life. For instance, journalism students could be encouraged to report from diverse communities, or sociology majors might undertake projects in unfamiliar environments. Finally, mentorship programs that pair students with professionals from various fields could offer insights into the complexities and nuances of real-world discourse, equipping them to navigate disagreements with maturity and grace.

## *Redefining Educational Integrity: Navigating the Minefield of Sensitivities and Truth*

**The Call for an Education System that Respects Sensitivities Without Compromising on Truth**

The modern education system finds itself at a crucial crossroads. On one side lies the demand for respect and consideration of various sensitivities, stemming from a society that is increasingly aware of marginalized voices and the pain of historical injustices. On the other, there's the unwavering demand for truth, rigor, and academic integrity. Bridging these two needs is challenging. Consider the controversial case from a few years back when certain universities in the US considered renaming buildings or removing statues tied to historically controversial figures. While the intent was to be more inclusive and avoid glorifying individuals with questionable legacies, critics argued that such moves could be seen as attempts to erase or rewrite history. Striking the right balance, where sensitivities are respected without diluting or distorting the truth, remains the Herculean task of modern educational institutions.

## Incorporating Multiple Perspectives Without Erasing Any

The diversification of curriculum is essential to ensure that students get a well-rounded understanding of history, literature, and societal structures. However, this comes with its own set of challenges. In efforts to include marginalized voices, there's a risk of sidelining or omitting established viewpoints. For instance, in the quest to diversify reading lists, if traditional texts (say Shakespeare or Hemingway) are excluded entirely in favor of more contemporary, diverse authors, students might miss out on understanding the historical evolution of literature. A true, holistic education should ensure that students appreciate the origins and journey of thought, even as they familiarize themselves with newer, diverse perspectives. The goal should be a mosaic of voices, where every tile has its unique place and importance.

## Laying the Foundation for a More Informed, Resilient, and Empathetic Generation

To prepare students for the real world, educational institutions need to adopt a tri-fold approach. Firstly, they should foster informed minds by exposing students to a full spectrum of ideas, even controversial ones, and teaching them the skills to discern, debate, and decide. Secondly, resilience needs to be built, not by shielding students from potentially offensive or challenging material, but by equipping them with the emotional and intellectual tools to grapple with such content maturely. Lastly, and most importantly, empathy should be at the core of education. While the debates around political correctness often hinge on what should or shouldn't be said, the deeper issue is about understanding and respect. The University of Chicago's letter to its incoming students in 2016 ignited debates when it took a stand against trigger warnings and intellectual safe spaces. Regardless of one's stance on the matter, the incident underscores the importance of fostering an environment where students are empathetic to others' experiences and viewpoints, while also being robust enough to engage with a world that won't always align with their perspectives.

# Chapter 6
# Artistic Sacrifices at the Altar of PC

## *The Silent Brush:*
## *Navigating the Tightrope of Artistic Expression*
## *in the Age of Political Correctness*

### The Increasing Prevalence of Self-Censorship in the Artistic Community

In a world dominated by social media, instant feedback, and the ever-present cancel culture, the realm of artistic expression has undergone a significant transformation. Once heralded as the bastion of free thought, where artists pushed boundaries and invited society to reexamine its norms, the artistic community now finds itself treading lightly, wary of the pitfalls of political incorrectness. While sensitivity and awareness are crucial, there's a growing concern that the pendulum may have swung too far, leading to a culture of self-censorship. This means that many artists preemptively tone down their work or avoid certain subjects entirely to escape potential backlash, even if the original intent was to engage audiences in a meaningful dialogue.

### Stories of Artists Altering or Abandoning Projects Due to Fear of Backlash

Stories of Artists Altering or Abandoning Projects Due to Fear of Backlash The cinematic landscape has often witnessed artists having to retrace their steps in light of prevailing PC standards. A notable instance can be seen in the realm of animation. The makers of the film "The Emoji Movie," for instance, came under scrutiny for their initial representation of certain characters and stereotypes. While the creators' intention was to produce a light-hearted comedy, several character portrayals were viewed as insensitive, leading to calls for changes. In response to the feedback, certain elements of the film were altered prior to its final release. Similarly, film directors and showrunners have frequently shared anecdotes of scenes they've altered, characters they've reimagined, or themes they've skirted to sidestep potential backlash. Such preemptive self-censorship highlights the lengths to which artists are going, often sacrificing their original vision, to appease a diverse and vocal global audience.

## The Consequences of a Stifled Creative Spirit on the Artistic Landscape

Art, at its core, is an exploration of the human experience in all its beauty, complexity, and at times, ugliness. When artists feel compelled to sanitize, modify, or dilute their expressions for fear of backlash, the entire artistic landscape stands to lose its richness and depth. Artistic movements historically have risen as reactions to societal norms and constraints, prompting viewers and readers to question, reflect, and sometimes, be uncomfortable. If artists continually operate within a restrictive framework, the world may be robbed of transformative pieces that challenge conventions and inspire change. Furthermore, this stifled environment risks fostering a generation of artists who are more concerned with external validation than genuine self-expression. In the long run, such a landscape may result in homogenized, safe, but ultimately uninspiring artistic outputs.

## *Represent or Resist:*
## *The Tightrope Walk of Modern Artistic Expression*

### The Modern-Day Challenges Faced by Creators in Representing Diverse Characters

The last decade has seen a surge in demand for representation in all forms of media, from literature to film. Diverse characters, with varied racial, cultural, and sexual identities, are not just requests from the audience; they have become expectations. Yet, with these expectations come a minefield of challenges for creators. Crafting a diverse character isn't simply about inclusion; it's about accurate and sensitive portrayal.

Artists face the dual pressures of ensuring representation, while simultaneously avoiding stereotypes. For some, this involves exhaustive research, consultation, and even reconsidering whether they are the right voice for a particular narrative. While these efforts aim to enhance authenticity, they sometimes lead to apprehension, with artists fearing they'll inadvertently misrepresent or misunderstand the very characters they hope to champion.

## Instances Where the Quest for Representation Compromises the Authenticity of a Narrative

In the rush to satisfy the clamor for representation, some creators inadvertently dilute the very essence of the narratives they pen. For example, in the realm of film and television, it's not uncommon to witness shows that, in an effort to check all boxes of diversity, introduce characters that seem forced or whose arcs don't mesh well with the central story. One such controversy arose with the film "The Great Wall", where actor Matt Damon was cast as the lead in a story set in ancient China. Many saw this as a blatant instance of "white-washing" and felt that it compromised the film's authenticity. The irony is that such attempts, which might be driven by the desire to appeal to a broader audience or to avoid the exclusion of certain groups, can result in narratives that seem disjointed or even disingenuous.

## Navigating the Thin Line Between Tokenism and Genuine Representation

Tokenism, the practice of making only a symbolic effort to be inclusive, especially by recruiting a small number of people from underrepresented groups, remains a pressing concern in today's media landscape. While the inclusion of diverse characters is celebrated, the shallow, one-dimensional portrayal of these characters is problematic. For example, a television show might introduce a character of a certain ethnicity or sexual orientation, but if that character's sole narrative purpose is to represent that diversity, with no real depth or development, it becomes a glaring case of tokenism. Artists, more than ever, need to ensure that their attempts at representation are not mere box-ticking exercises. Characters, regardless of their background, deserve depth, nuance, and agency in any narrative. The challenge for modern creators is to weave in diverse experiences organically, ensuring that every character's inclusion feels necessary and authentic to the story, rather than a begrudging nod to political correctness.

## *Art Under Siege:*
## *When Political Correctness Shadows Artistic License*

### Detailed Case Studies of Major Artworks, Films, and Literary Pieces That Faced PC-Related Criticisms

Art has often been a reflection of society, capturing the zeitgeist of its time. However, with the wave of political correctness, several major artworks have come under intense scrutiny and faced backlash. One striking instance was the 2017 controversy surrounding the painting "Open Casket" by Dana Schutz, displayed at the Whitney Biennial. The painting depicted the mutilated face of Emmett Till, a Black teenager lynched in 1955. Critics argued that Schutz, being a white artist, was appropriating Black pain and had no right to depict such a tragic and racially charged event. Similarly, films like "La La Land" were criticized for their portrayal (or lack thereof) of racial diversity and the jazz music scene. J.K. Rowling, too, faced backlash for her representation of Native American lore in her "History of Magic in North America" writings. These controversies, while varied in their specifics, underscore a shared theme: the conflict between an artist's right to free expression and societal expectations of sensitivity and correctness.

### Understanding the Societal Context and Reasons Behind the Controversies

The critiques against these artistic endeavors were not simply the results of a hypersensitive culture but are rooted in historical grievances and valid concerns about appropriation, misrepresentation, and erasure. To understand these controversies fully, one must delve into the societal contexts that birthed them. For instance, the objections to Schutz's "Open Casket" can be traced back to America's long and tumultuous history of racial tensions, where art depicting Black suffering was often commodified, devoid of its context. Similarly, criticisms of "La La Land" were magnified by Hollywood's ongoing struggles with diversity and representation. The challenge lies in recognizing the difference between constructive criticism, which seeks to rectify historical wrongs and prevent insensitivity, and overly zealous critique, which can stifle creativity and reduce complex issues to mere talking points.

## The Long-Term Implications of Such Challenges on Freedom of Expression

The contention between political correctness and art poses serious questions about the future of free expression. While it's essential to hold creators accountable for their representations, there's a tangible risk of artists becoming overly cautious, leading to a stifled, homogenized creative landscape. Fear of backlash might deter artists from exploring diverse themes or characters outside of their own lived experiences, thereby narrowing the scope of narratives we get to see and hear. Moreover, when artworks are removed, edited, or boycotted due to controversies, it raises the issue of whether modern society is, inadvertently, engaging in a form of cultural censorship. Balancing the legitimate concerns of underrepresented communities with the artist's freedom to create poses a significant challenge. Society must find a way to ensure that critique doesn't devolve into silencing and that artists can continue to challenge, provoke, and reflect the world in all its complexity.

## *Artistic Integrity vs. Public Sentiment: When the Canvas Clashes with the Crowd*

### Profiling Artists and Comedians Who've Been Pressured to Alter Their Vision

The past decade has witnessed a plethora of artists and comedians finding themselves ensnared in the crosshairs of public opinion due to perceived politically incorrect stances. One prominent example is comedian Kevin Hart, who stepped down from hosting the Oscars after past homophobic tweets resurfaced. While he had previously apologized for these statements, the immense pressure from the public and media caused him to relinquish the prestigious role. Similarly, visual artist Sam Durant faced vehement criticism for his sculpture titled "Scaffold," which combined design elements of seven gallows used in U.S. state-sanctioned executions, including the hanging of 38 Dakota men in 1862. The piece was intended as a critique of capital punishment, but many interpreted it as insensitive. Following discussions with Dakota elders, Durant agreed to dismantle the work. While both instances highlight artists' willingness to listen and amend, they also underscore the mounting pressures they face in a rapidly changing societal landscape.

### The Debate Over Whether Artistic Freedom Should Trump Societal Sensitivities

At the heart of these controversies lies a fundamental debate: should artistic freedom be inviolable, or should it yield to societal sensitivities? On one hand, defenders of artistic freedom argue that art, by its nature, should provoke, challenge, and even disturb. It is through these provocations that society is often prompted to introspect and evolve. Forcing artists to constantly walk on eggshells might stifle their creativity and mute the power of their commentary. On the flip side, proponents of societal sensitivities emphasize that artists should not be immune from the consequences of their expressions, especially when they tread into potentially harmful or traumatic territories for certain communities. They argue that with the platform artists possess comes the responsibility to be informed and respectful.

**Evaluating the Costs of an Art World Governed by the Whims of Public Opinion**

If artists constantly modify their work based on the prevailing winds of public sentiment, it could lead to a homogenized art world, devoid of controversy, challenge, or genuine innovation. Historically, many masterpieces that we revere today faced criticism in their time. Imagine if every artist from Van Gogh to Picasso curtailed their vision based on contemporary public opinion; the art world would undoubtedly be poorer for it. Furthermore, using public sentiment as a yardstick is problematic due to its fickleness. Today's celebrated opinion might be tomorrow's taboo. However, entirely dismissing public sentiment can alienate communities whose voices have been historically marginalized. The onus, perhaps, lies in finding a delicate balance where artists remain true to their vision without being dismissive of genuine concerns, and where audiences can critique without stifling or canceling.

## *The Commercialization Conundrum: Art, Profit, and Political Correctness*

**Delving into the Role of Profit and Marketability in Dictating Artistic Choices**

The age-old adage "art for art's sake" has long been overshadowed by commercial concerns, especially in the current age of rapidly consumable content. With globalization, artists and entertainment companies now cater to a broad and diverse audience. Thus, the choices they make are inevitably influenced by the demands of marketability. For instance, blockbuster films, which are designed for international releases, often steer clear of themes or depictions that could be deemed sensitive or offensive to a particular demographic. In some ways, this careful navigation is a nod to the diversity of global audiences. However, it can also mean compromising on an artist's original vision or diluting the content to make it palatable to the widest audience possible, even if it means sacrificing depth and nuance.

## How Commercial Pressures Further Complicate the Balance Between Creativity and Political Correctness

Navigating the maze of political correctness is challenging enough for artists. Add to this the pressures of profitability, and the path becomes even more intricate. Large production houses, publishing firms, and art galleries often find themselves at a crossroads where they must choose between endorsing a potentially controversial artistic endeavor and playing it safe to ensure returns on investment. For instance, a film with a hard-hitting message on racial tensions might be critically acclaimed for its boldness. Yet, studios might fear it's too polarizing for mass consumption and therefore opt for a more tempered narrative. This not only waters down the message but can also perpetuate stereotypes or offer a skewed representation of reality. Additionally, with social media's power, backlash against perceived insensitivity can translate into tangible economic losses, further intensifying the commercial pressures on artistic outputs.

## Instances Where the Commercial Angle Overshadowed Artistic Authenticity

The remake of Disney's "Snow White" serves as a glaring example of the tussle between commercial considerations and artistic authenticity. In a bid to avoid controversy, the title dropped "and the seven dwarves," and the film featured regular-sized men rather than dwarves. This decision, although commercially driven to avoid potential backlash, fundamentally altered the essence of a classic tale. By removing a key element of the narrative, the film not only distanced itself from its source material but also missed an opportunity to present a modern, sensitive portrayal of dwarves, which could have fostered inclusivity. Another example can be found in Hollywood's whitewashing trend, where roles specifically designed for actors of a particular ethnicity are given to white actors. Movies like "Ghost in the Shell," where Scarlett Johansson played a Japanese character, faced criticism for such casting choices. Behind this lies a commercial mindset: banking on established stars to guarantee box office success, even if it means sacrificing authenticity and risking cultural misrepresentation.

## *Safeguarding the Sanctuary of Art: Ensuring Freedom Amidst Societal Scrutiny*

### Proposing Safeguards to Ensure the Art World Remains a Space of Unbridled Creativity

The art world has traditionally been a realm of boundless imagination, a space where creators challenge societal norms and provoke thought. However, with increasing pressures to conform to politically correct standards, there's a growing need to safeguard this sanctuary. One way to ensure the art world remains a bastion of creativity is by strengthening platforms that support experimental and controversial art. These can be alternative galleries, underground theaters, or independent publishers who champion the avant-garde. Another safeguard is fostering an environment where critical discourse around art is encouraged, rather than suppressed. This means creating avenues for open debates and discussions, even if they touch on uncomfortable subjects. Furthermore, arts education should emphasize the importance of artistic freedom, teaching budding artists the value of pushing boundaries and the historical context of art as a tool of dissent and dialogue.

### Debating the Responsibilities Artists Have Towards Their Audience Versus Their Own Artistic Soul

The relationship between artists and their audience has always been a delicate dance. On one hand, artists create for self-expression, guided by their unique vision and personal truths. On the other, they are acutely aware of their audience, whose reactions can elevate or diminish their work's impact. But what happens when these two forces come into conflict? Some argue that in today's age of heightened sensitivities, artists have a responsibility to be more cautious and considerate. This perspective suggests that art, like any other form of communication, should not perpetuate harm or spread prejudice. However, others believe, rightly so, that it's precisely the artist's duty to challenge, to disturb the status quo, and to present unvarnished truths, even if they're uncomfortable. From this viewpoint, artistic integrity should not be compromised for the sake of appeasing an audience.

**Imagining a Future Where Art Can Be Both Reflective and Unrestricted**

Art has the potential to hold a mirror up to society, reflecting its beauty, flaws, complexities, and contradictions. But for art to truly serve this purpose, it needs the freedom to be both reflective and unrestricted. Imagine a future where artists can explore any theme, however controversial, without fear of backlash, but with an acute awareness of the societal implications of their work. In this envisioned world, artists would be equipped with both the sensitivity to approach subjects with nuance and the freedom to delve deep into them without censorship. Such a balance would not only enrich the artistic landscape but also foster a society more open to introspection and growth. This utopian future hinges on collective efforts—from educators, institutions, artists, and audiences—to value art as an essential tool for societal progression and to protect its sanctity against stifling pressures.

## *Reaffirming Art's Purpose:*
## *Holding Society Accountable Through Creative Expression*

**Revisiting the Essential Role of Art as Society's Mirror and Conscience**

From the intricate cave paintings of prehistoric times to the avant-garde performances of today, art has always been a reflection of society's core values, beliefs, and vulnerabilities. It doesn't just mirror society; it also serves as its conscience, highlighting its flaws, celebrating its triumphs, and exposing hidden truths. Historically, art has been instrumental in catalyzing social change, from Picasso's "Guernica" shining a light on the horrors of war to the music of the '60s inspiring a generation to demand peace and love. Political correctness, while rooted in noble intentions, can inadvertently dilute this pivotal role of art. When art is restrained, society loses a vital means of introspection. By revisiting and emphasizing art's role as both a mirror and a conscience, we remind ourselves of the larger social implications of restricting creative freedom.

## Championing the Idea that Art Should Challenge, Provoke, and Even Offend

Art is not meant to be a mere decorative piece or an innocuous form of entertainment. Its power lies in its ability to challenge the status quo, provoke thought, and, yes, sometimes even offend. The very nature of transformative art is that it doesn't pander to popular sentiment but pushes boundaries and compels its audience to think, feel, and question. Take Salman Rushdie's "The Satanic Verses," for instance. The novel sparked considerable outrage and controversy, leading to death threats against the author. While the book may have offended some, it also sparked global debates about freedom of expression, religion, and the role of art in society. By championing the idea that art should challenge and provoke, we underscore the importance of preserving a space where artists can express unfiltered truths, even if they are uncomfortable or unpopular.

## Proposing Ways to Educate Audiences About the Intrinsic Value of Artistic Freedom

To truly preserve the sanctity of art in the face of increasing political correctness, a crucial step is educating audiences about the intrinsic value of artistic freedom. This education should start early, integrated into school curricula, where students are taught about the historical and societal significance of controversial art pieces and the contexts in which they were created. Additionally, museums, galleries, and theaters can play a role by hosting events or discussions that delve into the value of artistic freedom, using past and present artworks as case studies. For instance, retrospective exhibitions of previously banned or censored art can serve as powerful reminders of the dangers of stifling creativity. Moreover, artists themselves, through open letters, interviews, and other platforms, can communicate their perspectives on the importance of unrestricted expression. By educating audiences on the value of artistic freedom, we not only cultivate appreciation but also fortify a collective defense against attempts to curb it.

# Chapter 7
# The World Watches:
# International Takes on PC

### *Not Just a Western Woe:*
### *Political Correctness Beyond Borders*

**Debunking the Myth That Political Correctness is Solely a Western Phenomenon**

Many believe political correctness to be a product of the Western world, particularly stemming from North American and European progressive movements. This perception paints political correctness as an issue exclusive to affluent societies grappling with their historical transgressions and current socio-cultural changes. However, this perspective is reductive and not wholly accurate. Political correctness, or variations of it, can be found in societies worldwide, even if they aren't labeled as such. For instance, in many East Asian countries, there's an emphasis on language and behavior that avoids causing offense or discomfort to others, not out of a written or imposed rule, but as a cultural norm ingrained for centuries. The rise of global communication tools, such as social media, has also facilitated the spread of political correctness ideals, adapting, and evolving in different socio-cultural contexts.

**Spotlighting Instances of PC Culture Across Different Continents**

Political correctness manifests differently across the globe, influenced by regional histories, cultures, and societal structures. In India, Bollywood—a massive film industry—has started to grapple with its portrayal of women, minorities, and certain controversial historical events, mirroring Hollywood's own reckoning with representation and sensitivity. In parts of Africa, where many countries have multi-ethnic and multi-religious societies, there's a heightened emphasis on respectful dialogue to maintain societal harmony. South Africa, with its apartheid history, particularly sees rigorous debates about language, representation, and historical recognition in its public spaces. Meanwhile, in Japan, there's an ongoing discourse on how certain marginalized groups, such as the Ainu or the Korean-Japanese population, should be represented in media and textbooks without perpetuating stereotypes.

## Exploring the Nuances and Variations in How PC is Received Worldwide

While the core principle of political correctness—promoting respectful and inclusive dialogue—remains consistent, its reception varies internationally. For example, in some countries, local iterations of political correctness align more with seeking national or cultural unity than with addressing minority rights. In other regions, PC is viewed through a post-colonial lens, where there's an added layer of sensitivity around not perpetuating narratives or stereotypes imposed by former colonizers.

However, this global spread also brings about challenges. In nations where freedom of expression is already limited, political correctness can be weaponized by authoritative regimes to further suppress dissent under the guise of maintaining "social harmony." China, for instance, has used the concept of "hurting the feelings of the Chinese people" as a mechanism to critique or suppress foreign criticism, effectively merging the lines between political correctness and state censorship. It's essential to discern between genuine attempts at fostering respect and inclusivity and manipulative strategies that use PC as a facade for control.

## *Cultural Contexts: The Global Palette of Political Correctness*

## The Fascinating Mosaic of Political Correctness as It Adapts to Different Cultural Backdrops

Political correctness, while rooted in a broad ideology of respect and inclusivity, is far from monolithic when we observe its manifestations worldwide. Instead, it forms a rich mosaic that continuously adapts to the cultural, historical, and social imperatives of different societies. For instance, while Western discourse on political correctness often revolves around race, gender, and sexuality, in some Asian contexts, the emphasis might shift towards age, hierarchy, or religious sensitivities. In the Middle East, PC discussions might center more intensely around religious respect and sectarian considerations. The parameters of what constitutes "offensive" or "respectful" are heavily influenced by each region's historical baggage, cultural values, and socio-political structures.

**Case Studies that Highlight the Relativity of What's Deemed "PC" Across Nations**

1. ***Thailand's Royal Sensitivities:*** Thailand, with its deep reverence for the monarchy, considers any negative or even constructive criticism of the royal family as not just politically incorrect but illegal. The nation's lèse-majesté laws make it a criminal offense to defame, insult, or threaten the king, queen, heir-apparent, or regent. Thus, while in many Western countries, political satires targeting leaders are common and acceptable, in Thailand, the same would be considered deeply disrespectful and punishable.

2. ***Japan's Burakumin:*** Japan's history with its "untouchable" class, known as the Burakumin, showcases another unique angle of political correctness. While modern Japanese society has largely integrated this minority, discussions or negative portrayals of the Burakumin in media and literature can be seen as politically incorrect. This form of PC doesn't stem from racial or religious differences but from historical class structures.

3. ***France's Secular Stance:*** France's approach to secularism and its manifestation in political correctness is also noteworthy. For example, the country's ban on face-covering veils in public spaces was justified as an assertion of French secular values, but critics argue it infringes on personal freedoms and targets Muslim

women. This balance between national secular identity and individual religious rights showcases the complexities of political correctness in diverse cultural contexts.

**The Universal Themes in Political Correctness and Their Unique Cultural Twists**

Despite the vast differences in how political correctness manifests across cultures, some universal themes underpin these discussions. These include the need for mutual respect, the avoidance of harm or offense, and the push for inclusivity. Yet, each culture imparts its unique twist to these themes. For example, the mutual respect that's advocated in Western PC culture regarding gender pronouns might find its counterpart in the Confucian-rooted societies of East Asia, which emphasize respect for elders in their linguistic structures and everyday interactions.

Similarly, while Western discourses around political correctness heavily push for inclusivity of marginalized racial or LGBTQ+ communities, societies with a strong caste or class system might focus their inclusivity debates around these social structures. The core remains consistent: recognizing historical wrongs and seeking a more just and equitable future. However, the path to that future is paved with cultural nuances, making the journey towards a globally accepted form of political correctness an intricate dance of understanding, adaptation, and mutual respect.

## *Resistance and Reception:*
## *The Global Divide on Political Correctness*

**Countries that Have Vehemently Resisted the Wave of Political Correctness**

The wave of political correctness has not been universally accepted, with some nations pushing back vehemently against what they perceive as a stifling of traditional values or an imposition of foreign cultural norms. Russia stands out as a key example. Under the leadership of Vladimir Putin, the nation has consistently resisted Western liberal ideologies, including the tenets of political correctness. Laws have been enacted that limit the rights and representation of the LGBTQ+ community, such as the infamous "gay propaganda" law which bans the promotion of non-traditional sexual relationships to minors. This resistance stems partly from the desire to champion traditional Orthodox Christian values and partly as a rejection of perceived Western cultural hegemony.

Similarly, in parts of the Middle East and Africa, many governments and societies resist political correctness in areas of gender rights and sexual orientation, often backed by conservative religious interpretations. In nations like Saudi Arabia and Uganda, there's significant resistance to liberalizing stances on women's rights and LGBTQ+ rights, respectively.

Hungary also presents an interesting case. Led by Viktor Orbán, the nation has resisted certain elements of political correctness, particularly surrounding issues of immigration and multiculturalism. Orbán's policies and rhetoric, which emphasize Christian values and Hungarian identity, have been seen by many as a rebuff to the broader wave of European political correctness.

**Nations that Have Enthusiastically Embraced PC and its Tenets**

Conversely, many countries have enthusiastically embraced the principles underpinning political correctness. Canada is a prime example, where policies and public discourses often emphasize multiculturalism, inclusivity, and reconciliation with Indigenous peoples. Prime Minister Justin Trudeau, for instance, has been vocal about gender equality, leading a cabinet with an equal number of men and women and championing feminist causes.

Sweden and Germany also stand out in Europe as nations that have proactively embraced many aspects of political correctness. Both countries have made significant strides in promoting gender equality, accepting refugees, and tackling issues related to racism and xenophobia. Particularly after the refugee crisis of 2015, German society underwent intense debates, and despite the rise of some right-wing sentiments, there remains a strong societal push towards political correctness in public discourse.

In Asia, Taiwan emerges as a beacon of political correctness in some respects, particularly concerning LGBTQ+ rights. The nation became the first in Asia to legalize same-sex marriage, showcasing its progressive stance in a continent where many countries remain conservative on such issues.

**Analyzing the Socio-Political Landscapes that Influence These Stances**

The acceptance or rejection of political correctness often ties back to a nation's socio-political landscape. For countries with histories of colonization, like many in Africa, political correctness can sometimes be seen as a new form of Western imperialism, imposing foreign values on traditional cultures. In nations with a strong central authority, like Russia or China, political correctness might be seen as a threat to state control, leading to resistance.

Religious beliefs also play a significant role. Conservative interpretations of religions can lead to resistance against what's perceived as the "liberal" values underpinning political correctness. In contrast, countries with secular traditions or more liberal religious interpretations might be more open to PC principles.

Economic factors also weigh in. Nations benefiting economically from global liberal orders and international partnerships might be more inclined to adopt politically correct stances, seeing them as part of a globalized, interconnected world. Meanwhile, countries feeling economically threatened might resist political correctness, viewing it as tied to global forces that are undermining their national well-being.

In all cases, the dance between political correctness and national identity is intricate, shaped by a confluence of historical, cultural, political, religious, and economic factors.

## *Eastern Sensibilities vs. Western PC: A Cultural Conundrum*

### Examining How Traditionally Collectivist Cultures Interact with Individualistic PC Ideals

Political correctness, as largely understood in the West, is rooted in individual rights, personal freedoms, and self-expression. Western societies, typically defined by their individualistic orientations, emphasize the rights of individuals to be who they are without facing discrimination or prejudice. On the other hand, many Eastern cultures prioritize the collective over the individual, which can sometimes be at odds with Western interpretations of PC.

In a collectivist society, the needs, values, and norms of the group (whether it's a family, community, or nation) often take precedence over individual desires or beliefs. Thus, a person might suppress their own feelings or needs for the perceived greater good of the collective. This dynamic complicates the integration of Western-style political correctness. For instance, while a Western perspective might champion an individual's right to express a non-traditional sexual orientation openly, a person in a collectivist society might feel pressured to suppress or hide this aspect of their identity to maintain harmony within their family or community.

Furthermore, some collectivist societies may see Western PC ideals as a form of cultural imperialism, imposing foreign concepts that disrupt native societal fabrics. The idea of individual rights above all can seem alien or even threatening to societal structures that have functioned harmoniously for millennia based on collective harmony.

**Exploring How Concepts Like Honor, Face, and Community Influence Perceptions of Political Correctness in Asian Contexts**

In many Eastern cultures, concepts like "honor," "saving face," and the broader community's well-being are deeply entrenched and influence everyday decisions and interactions. The idea of "face" in Chinese culture, for instance, is a multifaceted concept tied to respect, reputation, and social standing. Actions or behaviors that might "lose face" not only affect the individual but also their family, community, and sometimes even their broader ethnic or national group.

For example, consider a scenario where a young person in a traditional Asian community comes out as transgender. From a Western PC perspective, this individual should be supported and celebrated for their courage and authenticity. However, in the eyes of the local community, this revelation might be seen as bringing shame or dishonor to the family. The family, in turn, might prioritize the community's perception (maintaining face) over the individual's well-being or self-expression.

This is not to say that all Eastern or Asian cultures are monolithic or universally resistant to ideas of political correctness. Indeed, as global communication becomes more effortless, there's a blending of values and an evolution of thought in many parts of the world. But these deeply rooted cultural concepts do add layers of complexity to how PC is perceived and practiced in non-Western contexts.

**Debates and Dialogues Between East and West on the Best Way Forward**

The clash between Eastern sensibilities and Western PC ideals has sparked numerous debates and dialogues. Often, these debates are not simply about right or wrong but revolve around understanding, mutual respect, and finding a middle ground.

Some argue that Western nations sometimes approach political correctness with a kind of moral absolutism, failing to consider or respect non-Western perspectives. There's a risk of viewing Eastern cultures through a Western lens, branding them as "backward" or "oppressive" without fully understanding the cultural nuances at play.

Conversely, defenders of political correctness argue that certain universal human rights should transcend cultural boundaries. They hold that individuals everywhere, regardless of cultural or national context, should be free from discrimination, prejudice, and harm based on their identity.

Amid these debates, some Eastern nations have begun to incorporate or adapt PC principles in ways that fit their cultural contexts, signaling that it's possible to find a balance. For instance, South Korea's rapid modernization and globalization have led to increased LGBTQ+ visibility and rights, even as the nation grapples with its traditionally conservative values.

In essence, the dialogue between East and West on political correctness is emblematic of broader conversations about globalization, cultural exchange, and the challenges and opportunities they bring. Mutual respect, open-mindedness, and a willingness to learn from each other seem to be the keys to finding common ground.

## *PC and the Globalization Debate: The Web We Weave*

### Analyzing Whether the Spread of Political Correctness is a Byproduct of Globalization

Political correctness (PC) and globalization often find themselves mentioned in the same breath, leading many to posit that the spread of PC is an inevitable consequence of an increasingly interconnected world. With globalization comes the seamless flow of information, cultures, ideologies, and values across borders. In many instances, the values projected loudest and furthest tend to originate from dominant cultures or powerful nations. As a result, certain notions, including those of political correctness, often emanate from the West and spread to other parts of the world.

Yet, to claim that the spread of PC is solely a byproduct of globalization might be an oversimplification. Globalization is a vehicle, not the driver. While it facilitates the dissemination of ideas, local societies still retain the autonomy to accept, adapt, or reject these notions. For instance, while the idea of gender inclusivity may be gaining traction worldwide, its acceptance and the manner of its integration vary vastly from one country to another, showing that while globalization plays a role, it doesn't entirely dictate the narrative.

Furthermore, certain elements of PC may have parallels or antecedents in non-Western cultures, existing long before they became "globally" recognized. What globalization does is amplify, modify, and sometimes homogenize these concepts, giving the impression that they are novel imports.

## The Role of International Media, Films, and Pop Culture in Brainwashing Global PC Sentiments

The influence of international media, films, and pop culture cannot be underestimated in shaping global sentiments, including those about political correctness. The term "brainwashing" might sound severe, but there's no denying the persuasive power of global entertainment giants. For example, Hollywood, with its vast reach, often sets the tone for global cinematic narratives. When Hollywood adopts and promotes certain PC norms, these values can subtly become ingrained in the global psyche.

Consider the trend of increased diversity and representation in films and TV shows. While this is laudable, it sometimes risks presenting a sanitized or stereotypical view, especially when characters from varied backgrounds are shoehorned into narratives without depth or cultural accuracy. Such superficial representation can inadvertently shape global perceptions in skewed ways. A viewer from a different continent might form their entire understanding of a particular culture based on its portrayal in a Hollywood film, leading to misconceptions.

Moreover, global music icons and pop stars, with their millions of followers, have the power to influence not just musical tastes but also socio-cultural ideologies. Their endorsement or rejection of certain PC norms can sway large sections of their fan base, for better or worse.

## Debating the Merits and Drawbacks of a Unified Global Cultural Ethic

At the heart of the PC and globalization nexus lies an essential debate: Is a unified global cultural ethic desirable? On one hand, there are undeniable merits. A universal ethic could mean a world where certain fundamental values, like respect for all regardless of race, gender, or creed, are universally upheld. This could pave the way for greater global harmony and understanding, reducing cultural clashes and biases.

However, critics argue that the pursuit of a unified global cultural ethic, especially if it leans heavily on political correctness, risks the obliteration of unique cultural nuances and traditions. There's a danger of the world becoming a monolithic space where diverse voices and perspectives get drowned out in the din of a dominant narrative. For instance, while promoting gender equality is crucial, imposing a Western feminist perspective on a tribal community with its own unique gender dynamics might not be appropriate or effective.

Furthermore, a unified ethic, especially if it's shaped predominantly by powerful nations or entities, risks becoming a tool of cultural imperialism. The danger is not just about erasing diversity but also about whose version of "correctness" becomes the gold standard. Ideally, a global cultural ethic should emerge from collaborative dialogue, where every culture has an equal seat at the table, rather than being a top-down imposition.

## *Tradition vs. Transformation: Navigating the Tenuous Tightrope*

### Instances Where Traditional Practices Clash with PC Ideals

Historical and cultural practices often find themselves at loggerheads with modern politically correct ideals. While some traditions are celebrated for their uniqueness and antiquity, others are scrutinized for their perceived misalignment with contemporary values. One prominent example is the practice of bullfighting in Spain. For many Spaniards, bullfighting is not merely a sport but a deep-rooted cultural tradition that dates back centuries. It's seen as an art form, a dance between man and beast, rich with symbolic meaning. However, from a politically correct lens, especially in the context of animal rights, bullfighting is increasingly viewed as barbaric, inhumane, and archaic.

Another instance is the wearing of blackface during the Netherlands' Sinterklaas celebrations. While many Dutch people view 'Zwarte Piet' (Black Pete) as a harmless traditional character, there's a growing global sentiment that views the practice as a racist caricature. The tradition has consequently sparked heated debates within the country about cultural heritage versus global PC standards.

Lastly, consider female genital mutilation/cutting (FGM/C) prevalent in parts of Africa, the Middle East, and Asia. While some communities see it as a rite of passage and a means of preserving purity, many across the world, including activists from these regions, denounce it as a violation of women's rights.

### The Balance Between Respecting Cultural Heritage and Advocating for Progressive Change

Finding a balance between venerating cultural traditions and pushing for progressive change is a delicate endeavor. On one side of the spectrum, there's a danger of ethnocentrism—judging another culture solely by the values and standards of one's own culture. Doing so can lead to a dismissive attitude, where age-old traditions are casually labeled as "backward" without understanding their deeper context or significance.

On the other hand, under the guise of cultural relativism, there's a risk of turning a blind eye to practices that are objectively harmful, arguing that outsiders have no right to intervene or criticize. This perspective can hinder genuine progress and perpetuate harm.

For genuine balance, there must be an open dialogue where both sides are heard. Outsiders should approach with humility and a willingness to learn, while insiders, especially those adversely affected by certain traditions, should have the space to voice their concerns without fear of ostracization. This reciprocity can pave the way for a middle ground where traditions are honored but also critiqued and refined when necessary.

## Stories of Communities Evolving While Honoring Their Past

Evolution without erasure is indeed possible, and many communities worldwide offer heartening tales of how they've modernized their traditions without entirely discarding them. The Maasai people in parts of Kenya and Tanzania, traditionally known as lion hunters, offer a case in point. Recognizing the declining lion populations and the increasing global disdain for trophy hunting, some Maasai communities have shifted from lion hunting to lion protection. They've become guardians of the very beasts they once hunted, showcasing a profound transformation that's both progressive and deeply respectful of their warrior heritage.

In another example, some indigenous tribes in the Amazon, while maintaining their traditional ways of life, have incorporated modern technology, especially in the realm of conservation. Using drones and digital tools, they monitor deforestation and illegal activities in their territories, striking a balance between their ancient stewardship of the land and the demands of the modern world.

In Japan, the age-old art of Kintsugi, where broken pottery is repaired with gold, is used as a metaphor for embracing change. Modern artists use Kintsugi not just to restore antiques but to create entirely new art forms, symbolizing that while change is inevitable, it can be embraced in a way that pays homage to the past.

## *A World United or Divided:*
## *The Paradox of Political Correctness in International Relations*

### Political Correctness as a Barrier in International Relations

Political correctness, initially intended to foster inclusivity and respect, often inadvertently acts as a stumbling block in international relations. Instead of bridging gaps, PC culture can exacerbate divides by magnifying misunderstandings and creating an environment of walking on eggshells. Diplomats and leaders, in their attempts to be overtly sensitive, may sideline pressing issues to avoid appearing culturally insensitive.

Take, for example, the international conferences on climate change. While the core aim is to discuss tangible measures to mitigate global warming, these conferences can sometimes be overshadowed by arguments over terminologies or representation, detracting from the main objectives. Furthermore, countries often find themselves in defensive positions, trying to justify their cultural practices rather than focusing on collaborative problem-solving.

Another illustrative example is international trade negotiations. These dialogues, vital for global economic prosperity, often get sidetracked by debates on cultural appropriation and other PC concerns. Instead of fostering cooperation, they become a battleground of cultural egos, hampering progress.

## Envisioning a World Respecting Diverse Cultural Stances & Universal Human Rights Without PC

Imagine a world where cultures are respected not because of an imposed set of politically correct norms but because of genuine understanding and appreciation. In this envisioned world, the dialogue would be open and honest, devoid of pretensions. Leaders could confront hard truths without fear of being labeled insensitive, and nations could share their unique perspectives without being drowned out by the cacophony of political correctness.

This ideal world would prioritize universal human rights without the trappings of PC culture. For instance, the fight against gender discrimination would be approached not just from a Western feminist perspective but would incorporate voices from diverse cultural backgrounds, leading to more holistic solutions. Similarly, discussions on global health crises would be devoid of PC concerns and focus on tangible outcomes and shared responsibilities.

Such a world would recognize that every culture, no matter how different, brings something valuable to the table. The key would be mutual respect and understanding, not forced adherence to a one-size-fits-all PC doctrine.

## The Future of Political Correctness in a Rapidly Globalizing World

If political correctness continues unchecked in its current trajectory, the fabric of our global society risks becoming even more fragmented. The nuances of local cultures might be bulldozed by a monolithic PC culture, leading to a homogenized world where true diversity is superficial. Instead of celebrating unique cultural practices, societies might find themselves engaging in a performative dance of appearing "correct" at the cost of authenticity.

However, if the world decides to let go of stringent PC norms, we might witness a renaissance of genuine cultural exchange. Freed from the fear of mis-stepping, individuals and nations could engage in honest conversations, leading to deeper understanding and collaboration.

For example, international film festivals could become platforms where directors from diverse backgrounds showcase their unfiltered visions, giving audiences a true taste of global cinema. Similarly, global educational programs would emphasize learning from diverse sources without the concern of unintentionally offending someone.

In essence, a world without the overpowering shadow of political correctness would be one of unbridled creativity, collaboration, and genuine respect. Instead of being divided by what's "correct," societies would be united by mutual appreciation and shared goals.

# Chapter 8
# Political Correctness:
# The Unintended Consequences

## *The Road to Hell: From Noble Intentions to Overreach*

### The Noble Origins and Intentions of Political Correctness

The journey of political correctness started with a sincere intention: creating an inclusive society where every individual, regardless of their background, felt seen, heard, and respected. Rooted in the struggles of civil rights movements, gender equality drives, and other social reform initiatives, the primary goal of PC was to address historically marginalized groups' concerns. It was a call for empathy and understanding, a movement that sought to redress the scales that had long been imbalanced. Institutions, organizations, and influential figures championed the cause, recognizing its importance in forging a just society. Terms like 'sexist' or 'racist', once deemed radical, started gaining traction, compelling people to reflect on their beliefs and attitudes.

### The Gradual Shift from Core Values to Unexpected Pitfalls

However, as is often the case with movements that gain momentum, the very strength of political correctness—its dedication to sensitivity—became its vulnerability. What began as a tool to foster inclusivity started to morph into a weapon wielded by some to silence dissent or differing opinions. The focus shifted from promoting mutual respect to policing language with rigorous, sometimes arbitrary standards. This evolution, or rather devolution, brought with it the perils of groupthink, where questioning the dominant narrative became synonymous with cultural insensitivity or even bigotry.

A pivotal example of this shift is the trend of "cancel culture." Originated as a way to hold public figures accountable for genuinely problematic behavior, it has been increasingly weaponized to ostracize individuals based on minor infractions, past mistakes, or simply unpopular opinions. The case of a young adult author who faced severe backlash for her portrayal of certain cultures in her debut novel—even before its release—is emblematic of this. Succumbing to the pressure, she decided to delay the book's publication to make revisions, despite her original intentions of depicting a fictional universe.

## Highlighting Moments that Marked the Transition from Well-intended to Overreaching

Certain moments and incidents became flashpoints in the transformation of political correctness from a shield for the marginalized to a sometimes-blinding armor. Universities, once bastions of free thought and debate, became grounds for shutting down speakers whose views didn't align with a particular narrative. A notable instance occurred at a prestigious university when an invited guest speaker—a renowned figure with slightly conservative views—was disinvited due to student protests labeling him as 'dangerous'. Such episodes, which became increasingly common, marked a departure from the ethos of open discourse.

Similarly, the world of art and entertainment wasn't spared. Films, books, and music began receiving scrutiny not for their artistic merit but for their adherence to the ever-evolving standards of political correctness. The controversies around movies being deemed not representative enough or books facing backlash for not perfectly capturing the essence of a culture are testimonies to this trend.

These moments, among others, underscore the journey of political correctness. From its noble origins of ensuring a more inclusive and understanding society, it has, in certain spheres, transformed into a mechanism that, at times, stifles diversity of thought, expression, and genuine learning.

## Collateral Damage:
## The Unintended Fallout of Political Correctness

### Real-life Stories of Individuals and Groups Who Suffered Inadvertently Due to PC Norms

As political correctness seeped deeper into society, not everyone who was caught in its wave was a willful perpetrator of insensitive remarks. Many were merely bystanders or unintentional offenders who, due to the rapidly changing landscape of what was considered 'correct', found themselves in unexpected maelstroms of backlash. A poignant example is that of a professor who was forced to resign from his position after using a Chinese word that phonetically sounded like a racial slur in English during a linguistics lecture. The professor's intention was purely academic, aiming to demonstrate tonal variances in languages, but the backlash was swift and fierce, with students alleging that his choice was deliberately harmful.

Another instance involved a small business owner who faced boycott calls and online harassment due to a product's name, which was derived from her native language but was perceived as culturally insensitive by a different community. The name, which held sentimental value for the owner and was an homage to her roots, was suddenly at the center of a controversy she hadn't anticipated.

### The Fine Line Between Protecting Sentiments and "Causing" Unintentional Harm

Navigating the realm of political correctness feels like treading on a tightrope. On one side, there's the genuine need to ensure that public discourse remains respectful and considerate. On the other side, there's the risk of misconstruing innocent intentions and causing inadvertent harm. In a society hyper-aware and hyper-vigilant about perceived slights, the line between being protective and being overprotective blurs.

One need only think of artists who, out of fear of unintended transgressions, have begun to self-censor their works. Writers, for instance, are increasingly wary of crafting characters outside of their own ethnic or cultural background, fearing allegations of misrepresentation or cultural appropriation. While the intent is to prevent harm, the unintended result is often a curtailment of creative freedom and a narrowing of the artistic landscape.

## Evaluating if the Ends Justify the Means in These Scenarios

The pivotal question at the heart of these scenarios is: do the outcomes of strict political correctness norms, however well-intentioned, justify the adverse effects they occasionally produce? When an academic's career is abruptly ended over a misunderstood linguistic example or when an artist feels they must muzzle their creativity to fit within ever-narrowing confines, the cost of political correctness seems steep.

While it's undeniable that ensuring a respectful discourse, free from hate and prejudice, is imperative, it's equally vital to ensure that the methods employed to attain this goal don't inadvertently stifle freedom of expression and thought. The balance is delicate, and society must weigh the benefits of stringent PC norms against the potential fallout on unsuspecting individuals. The challenge lies in crafting a framework that protects without overburdening, that guides without dictating, and that educates without stifling.

## *A World Walking on Eggshells:*
## *Navigating the Delicate Terrain of Political Correctness*

**The Pervasive Anxiety and Stress That Now Dominates Public and Private Discourse**

In an era dominated by political correctness, one doesn't need to look far to witness the undercurrents of anxiety that lace both public and private conversations. There's a palpable tension in the air; from classrooms to boardrooms, from social media platforms to family dinner tables. Every word spoken, every tweet sent, every comment made is weighed, measured, and dissected for potential harm or offense. While the heart of this vigilance is well-intentioned, aiming to create an inclusive environment, it also breeds an environment of perpetual unease. Anecdotes abound of employees hesitant to engage in casual banter with coworkers, fearing unintentional offenses, or of students in classrooms too anxious to raise questions or challenge perspectives, lest they be deemed 'incorrect.'

**How the Fear of Offending Has Sometimes Paralyzed Genuine, Meaningful Conversation**

While fostering a sensitive environment is commendable, it comes at a cost—often, the cost of authentic, meaningful dialogue. Spaces that once buzzed with spirited debates, where divergent views clashed and coalesced to birth new perspectives, now sometimes echo with rehearsed, sanitized opinions. Take, for instance, the academic environment. Universities, traditionally bastions of free thought and expression, have seen instances where speakers are disinvited from events, not due to the lack of merit in their arguments, but due to fears of potential backlash. This culture of 'safe spaces'—while aiming to protect—sometimes does the opposite. Instead of preparing students to face, dissect, and debate differing viewpoints, it insulates them, creating echo chambers where only one 'right' perspective reverberates.

**The Psychological Toll on Individuals Constantly Self-Policing Their Language and Actions**

The continuous act of self-policing one's language, monitoring every word and gesture, doesn't come without a psychological price. Individuals are increasingly reporting feelings of exhaustion, frustration, and helplessness, trapped in a maze where the walls of 'correctness' keep shifting. A young author, for example, shared her experience of spending more time pondering the potential implications and misinterpretations of her characters and plotlines than on the actual art of storytelling. The sheer weight of potential backlash loomed larger than her creative spirit. Another account speaks of a teacher hesitating to comfort a distraught student with a simple pat on the back, fearful of how the gesture might be perceived.

This self-imposed vigilance, a perpetual state of alertness, can lead to mental fatigue, anxiety, and even a decreased sense of self-worth. For if one is constantly second-guessing oneself, parsing through every intention and action under a microscope, it becomes a challenge to remain confident and assertive in personal authenticity.

## *Overprotection and Resilience:*
## *Nurturing Grit in the Age of Political Correctness*

**The Science Behind Resilience and Its Development**

Resilience, often defined as the capacity to recover quickly from difficulties or adapt in the face of adversity, is not an inherent trait that some people simply possess, but rather it's a skill that can be cultivated. Scientific research suggests that the development of resilience is closely tied to exposure to manageable levels of stress or adversity. Like a muscle that strengthens with use, resilience grows when tested. From a neurological perspective, facing and navigating challenges can boost neuroplasticity, allowing the brain to adapt and forge new pathways. Psychologically, encountering adversity and overcoming it fosters a sense of self-efficacy, bolstering one's belief in their own abilities. The adage "What doesn't kill you makes you stronger" holds a grain of truth; overcoming obstacles or confronting and managing discomfort can bolster one's self-esteem and provide tools for future challenges.

## Case Studies Showing How Shielding Individuals from Adversity Will Inhibit Their Growth

While the intention behind overprotection might stem from a place of care and concern, in practice, it can have unforeseen repercussions. Consider a study from a prominent American university where students who had been shielded from opposing views and potential triggers in their early education found it exceptionally challenging to engage in open debates or confront unfamiliar perspectives in their higher studies. Their prior 'protected' environment hadn't equipped them with the tools to handle dissent, disagreement, or even mildly confrontational situations.

Another poignant example comes from a therapy group for young adults, where many participants expressed feeling ill-equipped to handle real-world challenges, attributing this to a lifetime of being shielded from any potential harm or distress, including exposure to 'uncomfortable' ideas or situations. One participant mentioned how a lack of exposure to failure made their first professional setback feel insurmountable, leading to disproportionate stress and anxiety.

## Discussing the Societal Costs of an Overprotected Generation

When an entire generation is ushered into adulthood with limited exposure to adversity or diverse perspectives, society stands on precarious grounds. The very fabric of democracy, which thrives on open dialogue, debate, and the free exchange of ideas, becomes vulnerable. When individuals are unaccustomed to handling disagreements or navigating challenges, the public discourse can devolve into polarized echo chambers, where each side is unable or unwilling to understand the other.

Moreover, an overprotected generation can lead to a workforce that's less innovative and adaptive. In a rapidly changing global landscape, adaptability and problem-solving are crucial skills. However, if individuals are conditioned to avoid discomfort or unfamiliar scenarios, their ability to think outside the box diminishes. Lastly, on a more personal level, overprotection can rob individuals of deeper, authentic connections. If one is always guarded, always wary of potential offenses or discomforts, the depth and quality of interpersonal relationships can suffer. After all, it's through shared challenges, disagreements, and resolutions that many human bonds are forged and strengthened.

## *Muting the Melting Pot:*
## *When Political Correctness Obstructs Cultural Integration*

### The American Ideal of a "Melting Pot" and How Extreme PC Might Impede True Cultural Integration

The United States, since its inception, has been fondly referred to as a "melting pot," a nation where diverse ethnicities, religions, and cultures merge together to form a unified whole. This ideal paints a picture of individuals from different backgrounds contributing their unique cultural essences, resulting in a rich and harmonious blend. However, extreme political correctness threatens this dynamic. Instead of fostering a sense of unity in diversity, an overzealous approach to PC often magnifies differences and places them in impenetrable silos. Rather than promoting the free exchange and blending of cultures, it can lead to a scenario where people are excessively cautious, afraid to share their traditions, or partake in others' for fear of being accused of insensitivity or cultural appropriation.

### Instances Where Diversity Was Celebrated in Theory but Stifled in Practice

On college campuses, which should ideally be bastions of free thought and cultural exchange, the overreach of political correctness has sometimes led to a paradoxical situation. For example, there was a case where a university's international cultural fair, meant to be a showcase of global traditions, became a hotbed of controversy. Participants were cautioned against wearing any traditional attire that wasn't from their direct heritage, leading to a subdued, guarded event, with many students choosing not to participate. The objective, while noble in intent—to prevent cultural appropriation—ended up creating an atmosphere where students were hesitant to share and learn about each other's backgrounds.

In another instance, a school district's decision to modify the content of a traditional holiday concert, stripping it of specific cultural and religious elements to make it more "inclusive," ironically led to a bland, homogenized performance. Instead of celebrating diversity, the event bypassed it altogether in an attempt to avoid potential offense.

## Striking the Balance Between Respect for Diversity and Assimilation

A society's strength lies in its ability to both cherish individual cultures and to integrate them into a cohesive whole. Respect for diversity means acknowledging and celebrating differences, but it shouldn't come at the cost of cultural exchange and shared experiences. Assimilation doesn't mean the obliteration of one's cultural identity but rather the creation of shared values and understandings.

Political correctness, in its ideal form, should guide this process, ensuring that cultural exchanges are respectful and done in the spirit of mutual appreciation. However, when taken to extremes, it can hinder the very integration it aims to protect. To strike the right balance, there's a need for open dialogue about what true respect for diversity looks like. This might mean creating spaces where individuals can share their traditions, explain their significance, and invite others to partake, all within an atmosphere of mutual respect and curiosity. In this way, the "melting pot" can continue to simmer, enriched by the contributions of all its constituents.

## *Compromising Authenticity:*
## *The Cost of Hyper-Political Correctness*

### How a Hyper-PC Environment Discourages Genuine Expressions of Culture, Belief, and Thought

A hyper-PC environment, with its stringent guidelines and unspoken rules, can inadvertently create a culture of restraint. This often manifests in individuals and communities feeling stifled, unable to express their genuine beliefs, cultural practices, or thoughts for fear of backlash. For example, authors, particularly those of minority backgrounds, have often reported feeling pressured to write stories that fit a particular narrative, sidelining their own experiences or views to cater to a broader audience's sensitivities. An artist, instead of delving into the nuanced complexities of their culture, might provide a sanitized version, fearing accusations of reinforcing stereotypes or being deemed "not authentic enough" by those outside their community.

Furthermore, in educational institutions, teachers might feel hesitant to delve deep into topics that are inherently controversial. Instead of fostering a space for constructive debate, there's an inclination to skim the surface, presenting an oversimplified version of events to avoid any potential pitfalls. This not only robs students of a comprehensive education but creates a generation ill-equipped to handle and discuss complexity.

### The Debate Between Maintaining an Authentic Voice and Adhering to Societal Standards

In an age dominated by social media, where public opinion can shift rapidly, the challenge for many is how to maintain an authentic voice while also navigating societal expectations and standards. Celebrities, influencers, and even everyday individuals find themselves at the crossroads of this debate. A singer wanting to experiment with music from another culture may second-guess their choice, worried about accusations of cultural appropriation. A writer might abandon a project that delves into the intricacies of another society's socio-political landscape, fearing they don't have the "right" to comment on it.

A poignant example can be drawn from the world of literature. There was a controversy surrounding a book which was pulled from publication after early readers deemed it inappropriate. The author had portrayed a culture different from her own, and despite her extensive research and consultation, faced backlash for perceived inaccuracies and insensitivities. This raised questions about who has the authority to write about certain topics and the fine line between appreciation and appropriation.

**Imagining a World Where Authenticity and Respect Can Coexist**

While the current climate might appear bleak, it's essential to envision a future where authenticity doesn't come at the cost of respect and vice versa. It starts with fostering environments—be it in educational institutions, workplaces, or public platforms—where open dialogue is encouraged. These spaces would emphasize the importance of intent, context, and the willingness to learn and adapt.

Consider, for instance, an international film festival that celebrates movies from around the world. Instead of merely showcasing them, there could be post-screening discussions where filmmakers explain their choices, answer questions, and engage in constructive debate. Such interactions would help audiences appreciate the authenticity behind the work while also providing creators with feedback in a respectful setting.

In conclusion, the goal shouldn't be to mute voices but to amplify them in a way that encourages mutual respect and understanding. By prioritizing dialogue over dismissal and curiosity over condemnation, a balance between authenticity and political correctness can be achieved.

## *Future Forecasts: The Path Ahead for Political Correctness*

### Predictions on the Future Trajectory of Political Correctness

As society continues to evolve, so too will the concept and execution of political correctness. With the current trend, there are concerns that the future of political correctness may veer into more extreme territories. This could potentially manifest in ever-stringening speech codes, an amplification of "cancel culture", and perhaps even legal repercussions for what is deemed politically incorrect speech or actions. An example that comes to mind is the increasing number of universities implementing "safe spaces" and "trigger warnings". While initially meant to protect vulnerable individuals, there's a looming danger that these concepts could be expanded and misused to shut down any discourse that challenges mainstream thought.

On the other hand, as with all trends, it's possible that society may reach a saturation point with political correctness. This could lead to a backlash, where individuals and communities rally against perceived constraints on their freedom of speech and expression. The rise of certain political movements and leaders who explicitly reject political correctness could be early indicators of this backlash.

### Exploring Potential Interventions or Shifts in Societal Thinking

For a more balanced future, interventions or shifts in societal thinking will be crucial. One potential intervention could be the re-education and reframing of what political correctness means. Instead of viewing it as a strict set of rules, it could be presented as guidelines meant to foster mutual respect. There's also a need for platforms that promote open dialogue, where individuals can discuss their viewpoints without the fear of backlash. A real-life example of this is the "red/blue workshops" held in the US, where people from opposite ends of the political spectrum come together to understand each other better.

Additionally, schools and institutions could play a significant role by introducing curricula that focus on critical thinking, empathy, and the importance of diverse perspectives. By equipping the younger generation with these skills, they'll be better prepared to navigate the complexities of political correctness and engage in constructive dialogue.

**Optimistic and Pessimistic Views of the Future Relationship Between Society and PC**

The optimistic view envisions a future where political correctness serves as a bridge rather than a barrier. In this scenario, society recognizes the value of empathy and respect, using the tenets of PC as a tool to achieve harmony. Differences are celebrated, but not to the extent where they hinder mutual understanding. There's a collective appreciation for the spirit behind political correctness, with most disagreements being resolved through dialogue rather than disdain.

Conversely, the pessimistic view paints a grimmer picture. Here, political correctness morphs into a form of Orwellian thought control, where individuals constantly self-censor out of fear. "Cancel culture" becomes rampant, stifling creativity and innovation. Society becomes more polarized, with individuals retreating into echo chambers that reinforce their existing beliefs, rather than challenge them.

In conclusion, the future relationship between society and PC will largely depend on collective choices. Will society use political correctness as a tool for unity, or will it become a divisive force? Only time will tell.

# Chapter 9
# The Age of Outrage and Perceived Victimhood

*Victimhood's Vicious Cycle:*
*A Dive into the Age of Outrage and Perceived Victimhood*

**The Sociological and Psychological Underpinnings of the Victim Mentality**

The victim mentality, from both a sociological and psychological standpoint, often stems from genuine experiences of victimization. However, when these experiences become a cornerstone of an individual's identity, they can create a self-perpetuating cycle where one views the world primarily through the lens of being a perpetual victim. This lens can distort perception, magnifying slights or misinterpretations into perceived acts of aggression or prejudice. Psychologically, this can be linked to cognitive distortions such as "catastrophizing" or "black and white" thinking. Sociologically, the continuous projection and reinforcement of a victim narrative in larger social groups can lead to collective memory, where past wrongs, either real or perceived, become ingrained in the shared history and identity of a group. An example of this is the contentious history of colonialism and its present-day implications in many countries. While the adverse effects and injustices of colonialism are undeniable, the challenge arises when present generations are continuously primed to view interactions, particularly with Western entities, through a lens of historical victimization.

**How the Constant Reinforcement of Victim Narratives Affects Personal and Societal Growth**

The frequent and pervasive reinforcement of victim narratives can create a culture of stunted personal and societal growth. When individuals view themselves primarily as victims, they may adopt a passive stance in life, feeling that external forces control their destiny. This can hinder personal agency, reducing the drive to take proactive steps towards self-improvement or change. Furthermore, if the broader society continuously affirms and emphasizes this victim identity, it can inhibit the community's collective drive for innovation and progress. For example, consider a society where narratives of past corporate exploitation dominate discussions about entrepreneurship. Potential entrepreneurs in this society might be hesitant to pursue their goals, fearing backlash or being labeled as exploiters.

Moreover, an overemphasis on victim narratives can lead to societal fragmentation. Instead of focusing on shared goals or commonalities, divisions based on perceived levels of victimization become paramount. This can lead to a competitive victimhood scenario, where different groups vie for the title of "most oppressed," often sidelining collaborative efforts for justice or reform.

**Examining How the Rise of Identity Politics Has Amplified the 'Victim' Mindset**

Identity politics, rooted in the justifiable need for marginalized groups to have representation and a voice, has become a double-edged sword. While it has been instrumental in bringing to light various systemic issues, it has also inadvertently amplified the 'victim' mindset in certain scenarios. As identity politics places emphasis on group identity over individuality, there's an inherent risk of homogenizing the experiences within these groups. This can lead to the perpetuation of certain narratives, including those of victimhood, even if they don't apply universally to all members of the group.

For instance, in some academic and social circles, there's been a noted trend where individuals feel pressured to conform to prevailing narratives of their identity group, even if their personal experiences diverge. A person from a historically marginalized background who might have a more positive or nuanced story to share might find themselves sidelined or accused of being "inauthentic" if they don't align with the dominant victim narrative.

Furthermore, the confluence of identity politics and social media has created an environment ripe for the spread and reinforcement of the victim mindset. Online echo chambers, where individuals are primarily exposed to views mirroring their own, can amplify feelings of victimization. In such spaces, nuanced discourse often gives way to outrage, further entrenching the victim mindset.

## *The Outrage Economy:*
## *Profits, Polarization, and the Loss of Nuance*

### Exploring How Modern Media, Including Social Media, Feeds Off, Profits From, and Amplifies Outrage

The modern media landscape, especially with the rise of social media platforms, has seen an explosion of content that seems to be crafted primarily for eliciting strong emotional responses. It's not just that outrage sells; it spreads. Due to algorithms designed to prioritize content that generates engagement, posts that trigger strong emotions, particularly anger and indignation, are more likely to be shared, commented on, and become viral. This dynamic encourages creators, influencers, and media outlets to produce more of such content, leading to an over-saturation of provocative headlines, clickbait articles, and incendiary opinions.

A notable example of this is the notorious "Twitter Cancel Culture." One misstep, sometimes taken out of context, can lead to an avalanche of condemnation, often resulting in individuals losing their careers, reputations, and social standing. While there are undoubtedly instances where such accountability is warranted, the instantaneous and often one-sided nature of these "online trials" highlights how quickly outrage can be ignited and manipulated on these platforms.

**The Economic Incentives Driving Sensationalism and Indignation**

In the age of the internet, where ad revenue is a significant source of income for many media platforms, there exists a clear economic incentive to prioritize sensationalism over substance. The more clicks, views, and shares a piece of content receives, the more ad impressions are generated, leading to increased revenue. This has given birth to what is colloquially referred to as "outrage journalism." Instead of prioritizing balanced reporting and nuanced analysis, there's a clear tilt towards stories that provoke, divide, and enrage, as these guarantee higher engagement.

Additionally, in an increasingly fragmented media environment, outlets are catering more and more to specific niches. These niches often revolve around specific ideological or political leanings. By continuously feeding these audiences content that aligns with and reinforces their pre-existing beliefs, while simultaneously provoking anger against opposing viewpoints, media outlets ensure viewer loyalty and consistent engagement.

**Real-World Consequences: Polarization, Misinformation, and the Decline of Nuanced Debate**

The consequences of the outrage economy are multifaceted and deeply concerning. One of the most evident impacts is the heightened polarization seen in many societies today. As people are continuously exposed to content that reinforces their worldview and demonizes the "other side," the middle ground begins to erode. This can lead to environments where compromise becomes a dirty word, and anyone not in full agreement with prevailing narratives is seen as an enemy.

Misinformation is another severe consequence. In the rush to be the first to break a story and generate outrage, fact-checking and thorough analysis often fall by the wayside. This has led to numerous instances where false or heavily biased information goes viral, only for corrections or retractions to be made quietly later on, after the damage has been done.

Lastly, the decline of nuanced debate is a tragedy in itself. Complex issues are reduced to sound bites, and the cacophony of outrage drowns out voices calling for understanding and dialogue. As a society, when the emphasis shifts from understanding issues in depth to merely reacting to them, we lose the capacity for growth, empathy, and true progress.

### *Real vs. Perceived Slights:*
### *Differentiating Genuine Grievances from Inflated Ones*

**Presenting Case Studies that Exemplify the Difference Between Genuine Grievances and Inflated Ones**

In today's outrage-driven culture, the lines between genuine grievances and perceived slights have increasingly become blurred. Let's explore two distinct cases to delineate this point further:

1. **Genuine Grievance:** The Black Lives Matter movement began in 2013 after the acquittal of Trayvon Martin's murderer. It has since highlighted systemic racism, especially in police practices, emphasizing concrete instances where Black individuals have been unjustly targeted, harmed, or killed due to racial prejudice. Their concerns have tangible, documented evidence, backed by a history of racial discrimination.

2. **Perceived Slight:** A university student in the US once claimed "cultural appropriation" when a fellow student wore traditional hoop earrings. The accuser felt that by wearing the earrings, the other student was appropriating a style "that belongs to the black and brown folks." While cultural sensitivity is essential, equating wearing earrings to deeper issues of cultural erasure or economic exploitation can dilute the severity of more pressing concerns.

**The Dangers of Equating Minor Inconveniences with Significant Societal Issues**

Equating minor inconveniences or misunderstandings with profound societal issues poses multiple dangers. For one, it risks trivializing genuine issues by placing them on the same level as minor slights. For instance, claiming emotional harm from a mispronounced name, while uncomfortable, isn't on par with systemic issues like wage gaps or racial profiling.

Furthermore, this kind of equivalence can lead to "compassion fatigue." When every issue, no matter its scale, is presented with the same level of intensity and urgency, the public becomes overwhelmed, and eventually, desensitized. This desensitization can make it harder for genuine problems, which require immediate attention and resources, to gain the traction they deserve.

Lastly, constantly being on the lookout for minor slights can create an environment of distrust. When individuals are continuously walking on eggshells, fearing they might inadvertently offend, it hinders open communication and relationship-building, which are crucial for societal cohesion.

**How the Diminishing of Actual Problems Can Be Counterproductive for Genuine Advocacy**

By amplifying perceived slights to the level of genuine grievances, the very cause that activists might be championing can suffer. Over-inflation issues can lead to public skepticism. When people continuously encounter what they deem to be overreactions, they might start to question the validity of other, more genuine issues raised by the same groups.

For example, if an activist group protests both the use of a racially insensitive term (a valid concern) and the serving of a non-authentic version of a cultural dish in a college cafeteria (a perceived slight), critics might dismiss the group's concerns altogether, thinking them overly sensitive.

Furthermore, diminishing real issues by focusing too heavily on perceived slights can divert resources, time, and attention away from addressing the root causes of significant problems. This not only hinders progress but can also cause disillusionment among activists and supporters who wish to see tangible change.

In the end, while it's crucial to advocate for cultural respect and understanding, it's equally vital to differentiate between genuine societal problems and minor inconveniences. Only by doing so can meaningful progress be achieved.

## *Schools and Universities: Enablers of the Outrage Culture?*

**Delving into the Academic Environment's Role in Cultivating and Reinforcing Perceived Victimhood**

Historically, schools and universities have been places of intellectual growth and debate, where students learn to think critically and challenge conventional wisdom. However, in recent decades, some argue that there's been a shift in this dynamic. There's a perception that these institutions, particularly universities, have transformed into echo chambers that, rather than fostering debate, actively stifle it in the name of avoiding offense.

One of the examples that often surfaces in this discussion is the disinviting of controversial speakers from university campuses. For instance, there have been instances where invited guest speakers with polarizing views were effectively "cancelled" by student protests, deeming their perspectives as "harmful" or "offensive". While the intention might be to protect certain groups from potential harm, critics argue that this approach not only infringes on free speech but also deprives students of the opportunity to confront and debate challenging ideas.

Moreover, the reinforcement of perceived victimhood can also be seen in classroom dynamics. Some professors, fearing backlash, have begun to avoid certain topics or are cautious about presenting them in ways that might offend. This self-censorship deprives students of a comprehensive education and fails to challenge them to think critically about complex issues.

**The Push for 'Safe Spaces' and Its Negative Implications**

The concept of "safe spaces" originated with noble intentions: to provide marginalized and vulnerable groups a sanctuary where they can express themselves freely without fear of judgment or harm. However, the application and interpretation of this concept have become subjects of contention.

Over time, the demand for safe spaces has grown to encompass not just physical locations but intellectual and emotional ones as well. This expanded definition has led to situations where anything perceived as a challenge or contrary opinion can be labeled as "unsafe". For example, there have been instances where literature classics were removed from syllabi because they might contain "triggering" content, or debates were shut down because they might make some participants "uncomfortable".

Critics argue that the overextension of the "safe space" concept fosters an environment where intellectual rigor is compromised. Instead of learning resilience and how to handle challenging ideas, students are shielded, leading to intellectual fragility.

**Analyzing How the Current Educational Paradigm Does Not Prepare Students for Real-World Challenges**

Schools and universities play a vital role in equipping students with the tools they need to navigate the complexities of the real world. However, when these institutions focus too heavily on protecting students from potentially "harmful" ideas, they might be setting them up for failure in the outside world.

In the real world, people are often confronted with ideas and opinions that challenge their beliefs and values. If students are conditioned to expect that these challenges can be avoided or shut down, they're ill-prepared to handle real-world conflicts, debates, and disagreements.

Moreover, by not exposing students to a diverse range of perspectives, schools and universities risk producing graduates with a narrow worldview. In professional settings, this can manifest as an inability to understand or empathize with clients, colleagues, or stakeholders from different backgrounds.

Lastly, there's a personal toll. Shielding students from challenges does them a disservice by not allowing them to develop resilience, critical thinking, and the ability to engage in constructive disagreement — all essential skills for personal and professional success in a diverse and interconnected world.

## The Erosion of Resilience in the Age of Outrage

### How Perpetual Outrage is Diminishing Our Collective Ability to Handle Adversity

The ethos of a society that promotes endurance and tenacity in the face of challenges seems to be dwindling in the age of perpetual outrage. With the amplification of every perceived slight and an increasing tendency to label challenging situations as harmful, our collective threshold for adversity appears to be decreasing. For example, whereas previous generations might have viewed certain hardships as rites of passage or opportunities for growth, contemporary culture often frames them as traumatic events that demand immediate redress.

Social media platforms play a pivotal role in this dynamic. These platforms allow for instantaneous reactions, often exacerbating the intensity of responses. For instance, a minor local incident can, within hours, transform into a global controversy, drawing thousands of comments, shares, and reactions. Instead of taking the time to process, reflect, and respond thoughtfully, the immediacy of the online environment promotes rash reactions, reinforcing a cycle of perpetual outrage.

Additionally, the normalization of outrage as a default response inhibits our collective ability to differentiate between major societal issues and minor inconveniences. When every incident evokes the same level of indignation, it becomes challenging to prioritize and address genuine societal challenges effectively.

**Showing How Societal Shifts Are Making Individuals More Fragile**

In tandem with the age of outrage, certain societal shifts seem to be nurturing a more fragile populace. The concept of "helicopter parenting," where parents hover over their children, closely monitoring and intervening in all aspects of their lives, is often cited as a culprit. Such parenting styles, while well-intentioned, might inadvertently shield children from the small failures and challenges necessary for developing resilience.

Consider, for instance, the rise in university students demanding trigger warnings for course content. While it's essential to be sensitive to trauma, critics argue that preemptively flagging all potentially distressing material could foster a generation unprepared for the unpredictability and challenges of real life.

Moreover, the conflation of emotional safety with physical safety is another indicator of growing fragility. While it's undeniable that certain words and ideas can cause emotional distress, equating them with physical harm can lead to an environment where intellectual challenges are viewed as actual threats, furthering the avoidance of discomfort and adversity.

**Balancing the Need to Address Real Issues with the Need to Foster Resilience**

Resilience is not about dismissing genuine issues or advocating for a "tough it out" mentality regardless of circumstances. It's about recognizing the difference between situations that demand intervention and those that present opportunities for growth. Addressing genuine traumas and societal issues is crucial, but so is ensuring that individuals are equipped with the tools to navigate life's inevitable challenges.

For example, while it's crucial to provide support for victims of serious traumas, it's equally vital to instill skills like critical thinking, emotional regulation, and coping mechanisms in the broader populace. These tools enable individuals to discern between genuine threats and mere discomforts, allowing them to confront and overcome adversities in a constructive manner.

Institutions like schools, families, and communities play a pivotal role in striking this balance. By fostering environments that both validate genuine concerns and promote resilience, society can cultivate a populace that is both empathetic to the struggles of others and equipped to face personal challenges head-on.

## *Emotions vs. Facts in the Age of Outrage*

**The Current Debate on Whether Emotions Should Override Factual Discourse**

In today's polarized landscape, there is an intense debate regarding the role of emotions in public discourse. Historically, factual discourse was viewed as a cornerstone of rational debates, where objective truths served as a guide for policy-making, decision-making, and societal discussions. However, the contemporary scene often witnesses emotions taking precedence over facts, driving narratives, and influencing outcomes. This shift is partly attributed to the evolution of digital media, where emotional content often garners more attention and virality than dry, fact-based reporting.

Consider, for instance, the rise of "clickbait" headlines and articles. These pieces are designed to evoke strong emotional reactions, often at the expense of nuanced and comprehensive coverage. This tilt towards emotional resonance over factual accuracy is not just limited to media outlets but is also observed in political campaigns, where catchy slogans often eclipse detailed policy discussions.

Moreover, the emphasis on personal experiences and anecdotal evidence, while invaluable for shedding light on individual struggles, can sometimes overshadow broader datasets. For instance, a heart-wrenching story of an individual might be leveraged to rally support for a cause, even if statistical data might suggest a different trend or solution.

**How Feelings-Driven Narratives Can Distort Reality**

Feelings-driven narratives, while powerful and impactful, carry the risk of distorting broader realities. Emotions are subjective, and when they become the primary lens through which events are interpreted, they can lead to a skewed perception of events. Take, for example, the concept of "moral panics," where society reacts to a perceived threat, often based on exaggerated or misinterpreted information, leading to disproportionate responses.

A classic example from history is the "Satanic Panic" of the 1980s and 90s in the United States. Rumors and fear-driven stories about satanic rituals and cults spread widely, leading to accusations, investigations, and even convictions, many of which were later debunked or overturned. Here, emotion-driven narratives, fueled by fear, led to a significant distortion of reality.

Furthermore, when emotions overshadow facts, they can inhibit constructive debates. If individuals are entrenched in their emotional beliefs and unwilling to consider objective data or alternative viewpoints, it becomes challenging to reach consensus or find middle ground. In such an environment, the emphasis shifts from "What is the truth?" to "Who can evoke the most potent emotional response?"

**Promoting a Balance Where Emotional Well-Being and Factual Integrity Can Coexist**

While the pitfalls of an emotion-driven society are evident, it's also essential to acknowledge the value of emotions in humanizing discussions and ensuring empathy. The challenge lies in achieving a balance where emotional well-being is respected without compromising factual integrity.

One way to promote this balance is through media literacy and education. If individuals are trained to critically evaluate information, discern between emotional appeals and factual data, and understand the mechanics of media manipulation, they can engage more productively in discussions.

Additionally, fostering spaces for open dialogue, where individuals can express their emotions and experiences while also being open to empirical data, can bridge the gap. Such spaces can be physical, like community town halls, or digital, like moderated online forums.

Lastly, there's a pressing need for influential voices – be it media personalities, political figures, or thought leaders – to lead by example. By ensuring their narratives are both emotionally authentic and factually grounded, they can pave the way for a society where emotions and facts harmoniously coexist.

## *Seeking Balance in the Age of Outrage*

**Proposing Ways to Reintroduce Balance, Nuance, and Perspective in Public Discourse Without the Need for PC**

In a landscape dominated by intense polarities, the need to restore balance, nuance, and perspective becomes increasingly critical. One primary way to achieve this is by focusing on education and media literacy. Empowering individuals with the tools to discern between biased narratives and balanced reporting can drastically shift the dynamics of public discourse. Media organizations must also be held to higher standards of objectivity, possibly through regulatory measures or public-driven campaigns demanding transparency and accountability.

Another avenue is prioritizing long-form content over bite-sized, sensationalized news. While the latter might cater to shrinking attention spans, it often sacrifices depth for brevity. Platforms like podcasts, extended interviews, and in-depth analysis can offer a more holistic view of issues, encouraging contemplation over impulsive reactions.

Lastly, the return to face-to-face dialogues cannot be stressed enough. The detachment provided by online platforms can often lead to dehumanizing exchanges, lacking the nuance, and understanding that personal interactions facilitate. Community gatherings, town hall meetings, and workshops focused on open dialogue can foster a sense of shared humanity, diluting the often antagonistic nature of virtual exchanges.

**Encouraging Critical Thinking and Empathy as Antidotes to Knee-Jerk Outrage**

Critical thinking and empathy are invaluable tools in navigating the tumultuous waters of public discourse. While the former allows individuals to process information objectively and skeptically, the latter ensures a compassionate approach, even towards opposing viewpoints. Schools and educational institutions should embed these skills into their curriculums, prioritizing their development alongside traditional academic achievements.

An example of this in action is the push for debate classes, where students learn to argue both sides of an issue, fostering an appreciation for diverse perspectives. Another is the emphasis on literature and narratives from diverse backgrounds, encouraging students to step into the shoes of characters vastly different from themselves, thereby cultivating empathy.

Furthermore, public figures, influencers, and community leaders can play a pivotal role. By modeling reasoned debate, showing respect for opposing views, and emphasizing the shared human experience over divisive issues, they can set the tone for their followers and communities.

## Promoting Solutions That Prioritize Healing, Well-Being, and Unity Over Division

To move beyond a culture steeped in outrage and division, the emphasis must shift to healing, well-being, and unity. Solutions must prioritize collective welfare over individual or group gains, ensuring that policies and narratives don't alienate or marginalize segments of the population.

One practical approach is the inclusion of conflict-resolution training in various spheres of life, from schools to workplaces. Skills like active listening, non-violent communication, and collaborative problem solving can drastically alter the way disagreements are approached and resolved.

Additionally, community-building activities that celebrate shared experiences, traditions, and values can foster a sense of unity. Local festivals, cultural exchanges, and communal projects can bring individuals from diverse backgrounds together, emphasizing their commonalities over differences.

Lastly, the role of art and media in healing cannot be underestimated. Films, music, literature, and other forms of artistic expression have the power to transcend boundaries, touch hearts, and bridge divides. By promoting and supporting art that seeks to unite rather than divide, society can take significant steps toward a more harmonious future.

# Chapter 10
# Towards a Future Without Overcorrection

## *Reimagining Respect in an Overcorrected World*

### Defining Genuine Respect Beyond Mere Appeasement or Pandering

In the age of political correctness, the definition of respect has, at times, been misshapen to resemble appeasement or pandering. However, genuine respect extends beyond superficial gestures or empty platitudes. True respect involves recognizing and appreciating the intrinsic value of individuals, regardless of their backgrounds, beliefs, or experiences. It means listening actively, even if one disagrees, and seeking understanding rather than mere agreement.

Often, what's presented as respect in the media or public discourse is a sanitized version, scrubbed clean of any potential disagreements. This form of "respect" can be restrictive, often stifling genuine interaction for fear of causing offense. For instance, avoiding discussions about race or religion to prevent potential discomfort, while well-intentioned, can hinder deeper understanding and genuine connection between individuals of different backgrounds.

Contrarily, genuine respect invites open dialogue and welcomes diverse perspectives, understanding that disagreements or discomforts can be the breeding grounds for growth and enlightenment when approached with an open heart and mind.

### Exploring Cultural, Regional, and Generational Variations in Understanding Respect

Respect, as a concept, is fluid and its interpretation varies across cultures, regions, and generations. In some cultures, for example, maintaining eye contact is seen as a sign of attentiveness and respect, while in others, it's perceived as confrontational or rude. Similarly, certain gestures like handshakes or bows carry different weights and meanings in various regions.

Generationally, respect dynamics have evolved significantly. Older generations might equate respect with strict adherence to hierarchies and established protocols. For them, respect might mean never questioning authority or elders, and always adhering to tradition. Meanwhile, younger generations, influenced by globalized communication and more egalitarian ideals, might view respect as mutual and not tied strictly to age or status. For instance, they might value open dialogue, transparency, and mutual understanding as core tenets of respect.

Understanding these nuances is crucial, especially in a globalized world. Without this awareness, what one person perceives as a respectful gesture might be seen as a slight or ignorance by another, leading to unnecessary misunderstandings.

## Case Studies of Communities or Nations That Have Achieved Harmonious Balance

One remarkable case study is Singapore, a small nation that's a melting pot of ethnicities, religions, and cultures. Despite its diverse makeup, Singapore has largely managed to maintain racial and religious harmony. This achievement is, in part, due to its strict laws against "hate" speech and its active promotion of multiculturalism. Schools, for example, teach in English, but students are also required to learn a "mother tongue" associated with their ethnicity, promoting bilingualism and biculturalism.

Another example can be found in the city of Cordoba in Spain. During the Middle Ages, Cordoba stood as a beacon of interfaith harmony, where Muslims, Christians, and Jews coexisted and collaborated in fields ranging from philosophy to science. This harmony was not born out of suppression of differences but rather an acknowledgment and appreciation of them.

Lastly, the indigenous Maori of New Zealand have been successful in integrating into modern New Zealand society while retaining their unique cultural identity. The Treaty of Waitangi, signed in 1840, laid the groundwork for Maori rights in the country. Today, the Maori language is celebrated, Haka performances are a source of national pride, and Maori customs and values are intertwined with New Zealand's national identity. This harmonious balance was achieved through mutual respect, dialogue, and understanding between the indigenous community and later settlers.

## Correcting Overcorrection in the Age of Political Correctness

### Identifying Key Areas Where Political Correctness Has Overreached Its Intended Purpose

One of the first domains in which political correctness appears to have overstepped is comedy. Historically, humor has served as a mirror to society, highlighting its foibles, absurdities, and inequities. Comedians, for instance, like Lenny Bruce or George Carlin, used their platforms to challenge societal norms and provoke thought. However, with the rise of political correctness, comedians are frequently criticized for their content, potentially stifling creativity and limiting their ability to satirize contemporary issues. The once revered space of comedy, which thrived on pushing boundaries and challenging conventions, finds itself walking on eggshells.

In academia, too, political correctness can sometimes hamper the free exchange of ideas. Campuses across the West, traditionally arenas for vigorous debate and dissent, have witnessed disruptions or disinvitations of speakers whose views challenge the prevailing orthodoxy. While the intention might be to protect students from potentially harmful ideas, such actions risk creating intellectual echo chambers, depriving students of the opportunity to engage with diverse viewpoints.

Moreover, in the professional sphere, the quest for inclusivity has occasionally manifested in the form of tokenism. Rather than genuinely promoting diversity and understanding, some organizations seem more intent on ticking boxes, prioritizing surface-level diversity over substantive inclusion. This results in qualified individuals being overlooked and a diluted understanding of what true diversity entails.

## Proposing Actionable Solutions and Interventions to Recalibrate Societal Norms

To begin the process of recalibration, it's essential to differentiate between intent and impact. By focusing on the intention behind words or actions, it becomes easier to discern whether something was genuinely harmful or merely a misstep. Educating individuals about cultural sensitivities, without punishing inadvertent offenses, can be a more constructive approach.

Institutional measures can also play a vital role. Academic institutions, for example, could establish clearer guidelines on freedom of speech versus "hate" speech, ensuring that campuses remain open to diverse views without compromising on student safety. They can also actively promote debates, encouraging students to engage with opposing perspectives in a controlled and respectful environment.

Businesses and organizations, on the other hand, could benefit from diversity and inclusion training that goes beyond mere tokenism. This involves moving past mere representation to ensuring that all voices are genuinely heard and valued, creating environments where diverse perspectives can genuinely thrive.

## Promoting Dialogue, Understanding, and Mutual Growth

At the heart of any recalibration must be a commitment to dialogue. This entails creating safe spaces where individuals can express their views, ask questions, and learn without fear of retribution. Encouraging conversations, even uncomfortable ones, can lead to deeper understanding and empathy. By sharing personal stories and experiences, individuals can foster mutual growth and bridge the gaps that divide them.

Moreover, leveraging media and popular culture can also be instrumental in promoting understanding. By showcasing diverse stories, experiences, and perspectives, media can play a role in normalizing differences and highlighting shared human experiences. Such exposure can challenge preconceived notions and facilitate a more nuanced understanding of diverse communities.

Lastly, grassroots movements and community initiatives can play a crucial role in fostering dialogue and understanding at a local level. By organizing town halls, workshops, or even informal meet-ups, communities can provide platforms for their members to engage, understand, and grow together, moving towards a future where respect and understanding triumph over mere political correctness.

## *Triggers and Tolerance in the Age of Political Correctness*

### Educating the Public About the Science and Psychology of Triggers

The concept of triggers — stimuli that provoke intense emotional reactions, often rooted in trauma or past negative experiences — has gained widespread recognition in recent years. However, its popularization has led to both genuine understanding and, unfortunately, misuse. Originally, the term referred to sensations or events that would evoke traumatic memories, especially in individuals with PTSD. Yet, today, it's not uncommon to find people labeling anything unpleasant or slightly disagreeable as a "trigger," thereby diluting the profound severity of actual traumatic triggers.

This misapprehension about triggers is concerning for several reasons. For one, trivializing the term diminishes the genuine experiences of individuals who suffer from trauma. When everything becomes a "trigger," it becomes challenging to discern and accommodate severe cases that require immediate attention and care. For instance, a war veteran might be genuinely triggered by loud noises reminiscent of gunfire, leading to debilitating flashbacks, while another person might claim to be "triggered" by a minor disagreement or a passing comment.

As such, it's imperative to educate the public about the actual science and psychology behind triggers. This includes understanding the difference between a genuine traumatic response and mere discomfort. It's essential for schools, media outlets, and public figures to disseminate accurate information and discourage the trivialization of such a vital term.

## Encouraging Societal Norms Where Individuals Manage Their Sensitivities While Being Compassionate to Others

Managing sensitivities is a delicate balancing act. On one hand, it's crucial to respect and understand the genuine discomfort or pain of others. On the other hand, it's equally important for individuals to take responsibility for their emotional responses and not expect the world to continuously accommodate their personal discomforts. There's a significant difference between requesting a classroom warning for graphic content that could retraumatize a sexual assault survivor, and demanding the complete removal of classic literature because it contains outdated or disagreeable perspectives.

Promoting a culture of resilience, self-awareness, and personal responsibility can be beneficial. This would entail empowering individuals with tools to manage their reactions, discern between genuine triggers and mere inconveniences, and seek professional help when necessary. For instance, therapy, meditation, and mindfulness techniques can help individuals navigate their emotional landscape more effectively.

At the same time, fostering compassion and empathy in society is paramount. It's possible to be understanding of others' sensitivities without necessarily pandering to every demand. Finding this balance requires open dialogue, education, and a mutual desire to coexist harmoniously, even in the face of disagreement or discomfort.

**Exploring Global Practices on Emotional Intelligence and Tolerance**

Different cultures around the world have unique approaches to emotional intelligence and tolerance. For instance, certain Eastern philosophies emphasize inner peace, acceptance, and detachment from external events. In places like Bhutan, which prioritizes Gross National Happiness over GDP, there's a societal emphasis on emotional and spiritual well-being.

Scandinavian countries, known for their high quality of life rankings, incorporate societal norms that emphasize community, understanding, and mutual respect. Their education systems, for example, are often geared towards fostering critical thinking, self-awareness, and emotional intelligence from a young age.

On the other hand, nations that have experienced significant turmoil or conflict may develop a collective resilience and understanding of trauma. In post-apartheid South Africa, the Truth and Reconciliation Commission sought to heal the nation's wounds through dialogue, understanding, and shared narratives, showcasing a remarkable national exercise in emotional intelligence and tolerance.

Such global practices offer valuable insights. By studying and potentially integrating these diverse approaches, societies can develop richer, more holistic strategies to nurture emotional intelligence, cultivate tolerance, and navigate the complexities of triggers in an age dominated by political correctness.

## The Importance of Discerning Intention in a Politically Correct Landscape

**The Debate Between Judging Actions Based on Their Intent Versus Their Impact**

In recent years, a significant debate has emerged over whether one should judge actions based on their intent or their impact. This discussion is particularly pertinent in the era of political correctness, where a seemingly innocent comment can be perceived as offensive, leading to potential backlash. Those in the "intent" camp argue that if a person didn't mean any harm, they shouldn't be held accountable to the same degree as someone who deliberately sets out to offend. Conversely, proponents of the "impact" perspective assert that it's the effect of the action or words that matters most, regardless of the intent behind them.

One well-publicized example revolves around comedians and their jokes. Comedians often tread a fine line between satire and offense. A joke, even if not intended to harm, might deeply hurt a particular group or individual. Ricky Gervais, a prominent comedian, has frequently commented on this debate, asserting that jokes shouldn't be censored based on potential harm if there was no malicious intent behind them. However, critics argue that such a stance is dismissive of genuine pain and distress certain jokes can induce, regardless of the comedian's intentions.

The crux of the matter is the complexity of human communication and perception. While intent can provide context, it doesn't always mitigate harm. But should individuals live in fear of inadvertently causing offense, even when their intentions are pure? It's a delicate balance to strike, especially in an age where every misstep can be magnified on the global stage of social media.

## Highlighting Cultural and Individual Variations in Communication Styles

Cultural and individual differences in communication styles can further complicate the intent versus impact debate. What's considered polite or commonplace in one culture might be perceived as rude or inappropriate in another. For example, in some Eastern cultures, direct eye contact might be viewed as aggressive or confrontational, while in Western societies, it's often seen as a sign of confidence and honesty.

Furthermore, some cultures prioritize indirect or high-context communication, where much of the message is conveyed through non-verbal cues or is understood based on cultural context. In contrast, other cultures value direct or low-context communication, where messages are expressed explicitly through words. These variations can lead to misunderstandings. An individual from a high-context culture might perceive a direct statement from someone of a low-context culture as brash or insensitive, even if it was not intended that way.

Historically, many diplomatic misunderstandings have arisen from these cultural differences in communication. For instance, during international negotiations, the subtleties of "yes" in various cultures can lead to misinterpretations. In some contexts, "yes" might mean "I understand" rather than "I agree," leading to potential confusion.

**Tools and Techniques to Discern and Clarify Intentions in Daily Interactions**

Given the intricacies of human interaction, it's crucial to equip individuals with tools and techniques to discern and clarify intentions. One effective method is the practice of active listening. This involves fully concentrating, understanding, and responding to what the other person is saying, rather than merely waiting for one's turn to speak. By giving undivided attention, one can pick up on subtle cues and nuances, paving the way for clearer understanding.

Another useful technique is the principle of charity, particularly in debates or disagreements. This means interpreting another person's statement in its best, most reasonable form, rather than jumping to negative conclusions. For instance, if someone makes a potentially offensive remark, it might be beneficial to ask them to clarify or elaborate, giving them the opportunity to express their intention more clearly.

Additionally, educating oneself on different cultural norms and communication styles can be immensely beneficial. This doesn't mean one has to become an expert in every culture, but having a foundational understanding can prevent many misunderstandings. Workshops, travel experiences, or even reading can provide these insights.

In the digital age, where face-to-face nuances are often lost in text, emojis and GIFs have become tools to convey tone and intention. While they might seem trivial, they play a significant role in providing context in online interactions.

Ultimately, discerning intention requires a blend of empathy, education, and active effort. In a world quick to judge, taking that extra moment to understand can bridge divides and reduce unnecessary conflict.

## *Introducing Critical Thinking, Empathy, and Communication in Modern Education*

### The Argument for Making Critical Thinking, Empathy, and Communication Pillars of Modern Education

The current state of global discourse, influenced in part by the extremes of political correctness, underscores the pressing need to incorporate critical thinking, empathy, and effective communication into the core of modern education. Critical thinking allows individuals to dissect information, discerning fact from fiction, and helping them navigate the complexities of today's information-saturated world. With the rise of misinformation and echo chambers, critical thinking serves as an antidote, allowing individuals to question, validate, and form well-rounded views.

Empathy, on the other hand, forms the emotional backbone of any civilized society. In the divisive climate fostered by extreme political correctness, empathy allows individuals to understand and respect perspectives different from their own, even if they don't necessarily agree with them. It's not about endorsing every viewpoint, but about acknowledging the emotional and experiential validity behind them.

Lastly, communication serves as the bridge connecting critical thinking and empathy. Even the most empathetic, well-reasoned perspective is of little value if it cannot be communicated effectively. In an age where "cancel culture" can amplify minor misunderstandings, the ability to articulate thoughts clearly and respectfully has never been more vital.

**Real-world Benefits of Equipping the Younger Generation with Critical Thinking, Empathy, and Communication Skills**

By instilling these core principles in the younger generation, society stands to reap manifold benefits. Critical thinkers are better equipped to sift through the deluge of information and misinformation that characterizes the digital age. This skill protects them from being swayed by extremist views or false narratives and promotes a more informed and balanced society. For instance, amidst a contentious political election, young voters equipped with critical thinking skills can delve beyond sensational headlines, evaluating policies and candidates on their actual merits rather than on media-driven narratives.

Empathy fosters a more inclusive and harmonious society. In recent years, there have been numerous accounts of college campuses erupting in protests, sometimes violent, over controversial speakers or ideas. While the right to protest is essential, an empathetic approach might lead to more constructive dialogues rather than confrontations. Students might seek to understand the roots of opposing views and engage in open debates, leading to mutual growth and understanding.

Effective communication complements the other two pillars. In the workplace, for instance, teams that communicate effectively are more productive, have higher morale, and report better job satisfaction. On a societal scale, clearer communication can defuse potential conflicts, foster collaboration, and pave the way for innovative solutions to pressing challenges.

**Action Plans for Integrating These Principles into Curriculums Worldwide**

Given the global significance of these skills, there's a compelling argument for their integration into curriculums worldwide. Here are some actionable strategies:

1.  **Revamp Curriculum Content:** Introduce subjects or modules dedicated explicitly to critical thinking, empathy, and communication. For instance, schools could offer courses in logical reasoning, debate, and emotional intelligence, ensuring students have ample opportunities to practice and hone these skills.

2.  **Interactive Learning:** Move beyond traditional rote learning. Encourage group projects, debates, and role-playing exercises. For instance, a classroom could simulate a United Nations conference where students represent different countries, fostering both research (critical thinking), understanding diverse perspectives (empathy), and articulating their positions (communication).

3.  **Teacher Training:** Invest in training educators to integrate these principles into their teaching methodologies, regardless of the subject they teach. A math teacher can emphasize logical reasoning, while a literature teacher can focus on understanding characters' emotions and motivations.

4.  **Technology Integration:** Leverage technology to expose students to a plethora of perspectives. Platforms like Khan Academy or Coursera could introduce modules on these principles. Virtual exchange programs, where students interact with peers from different cultures online, can foster global empathy and improve communication skills.

5.  **Evaluation Metrics:** Update examination and grading systems to reflect these skills. Instead of merely focusing on memorization,

assessments could evaluate students on their ability to reason, understand diverse viewpoints, and communicate effectively.

While the road to global curriculum reform is long and fraught with challenges, the pressing need for a more reasoned, empathetic, and articulate society makes the journey not just worthwhile but essential.

## *Lessons from History*

### A Brief Look at Historical Instances of Societal Overcorrection and Their Outcomes

Throughout history, societies have often veered from one extreme to another, reacting to perceived injustices or inequalities by overcorrecting and, in the process, creating new sets of challenges. One of the most iconic instances is the French Revolution. What began as a legitimate demand for equality and representation turned into the Reign of Terror, where thousands were executed for perceived counter-revolutionary beliefs. This overcorrection resulted in the emergence of a new autocracy under Napoleon Bonaparte.

Another example can be observed in the Prohibition era in the United States. In response to the very real societal problems associated with alcohol consumption, the 18th Amendment was ratified in 1919, prohibiting the production, sale, and transport of alcoholic beverages. However, rather than curbing the adverse effects of alcohol, Prohibition led to the rise of organized crime, illegal speakeasies, and widespread corruption. The intent behind the movement was commendable, but its overzealous application exacerbated societal issues.

China's Cultural Revolution (1966-1976) stands as another testament to the dangers of overcorrection. Initiated by Mao Zedong, the goal was to preserve and propagate communist ideology by removing capitalist, traditional, and cultural elements from Chinese society. This led to a decade of chaos, with countless historical relics destroyed, cultural and religious sites ransacked, and millions persecuted.

**Drawing Parallels and Lessons for Our Current Predicament**

Drawing from these historical overcorrections, there are clear parallels to the contemporary issues surrounding political correctness. Just as the French Revolution initially sought equality but led to the Reign of Terror, extreme forms of political correctness, while initially rooted in the noble pursuit of inclusivity and understanding, can lead to societal divisions, suppression of free speech, and even ostracism of those with differing opinions.

Similarly, the Prohibition era's intent to improve societal well-being mirrors the intentions behind political correctness. However, just as Prohibition inadvertently amplified the very issues it sought to address, an overzealous approach to political correctness can inadvertently amplify division, misunderstanding, and even resentment.

The Cultural Revolution's efforts to purge society of perceived detrimental influences and establish a uniform ideology finds its reflection in extreme facets of political correctness that seek to eliminate any form of dissent or alternative perspective, stressing conformity over individual thought.

**Emphasizing the Cyclical Nature of Societal Shifts and the Importance of Mindful Progress**

Historical patterns suggest a cyclical nature in societal attitudes, swinging like a pendulum between extremes before finding equilibrium. The extremes of political correctness may be seen as a reaction to previous societal norms that marginalized or dismissed certain groups or perspectives. Recognizing this cyclical pattern is crucial as it offers hope that equilibrium, once lost, can be regained.

However, history also provides a cautionary tale. The pendulum swings, while natural, can have dire consequences if not tempered with mindfulness and a keen awareness of the broader picture. It emphasizes the importance of progress that is reflective, inclusive, and considerate of the diverse fabric of society.

While it's essential to correct past injustices and promote a more inclusive society, the lessons from history underline the importance of doing so with care and caution. Pushing too hard or too fast, without considering potential consequences, can lead to the very divisiveness and strife that such movements aim to eradicate. Mindful progress, informed by history, can guide societies towards a more balanced, harmonious future.

## *The Way Forward*

### Envisioning a World Where Mutual Respect, Understanding, and Coexistence Reign Supreme

In an ideal world, individuals would understand and appreciate the diverse tapestry of human experiences, cultures, and beliefs. Such a world would be devoid of assumptions based on mere external appearances or singular narratives. The danger of a single story, as Nigerian author Chimamanda Ngozi Adichie once described, is that it reduces complex beings to a single, often misguided, narrative. In this envisaged world, conversations would not begin from a point of suspicion, but from genuine curiosity and a desire to understand. Here, respect is not merely a result of fear of backlash or societal pressure but springs from a genuine understanding and appreciation of the myriad paths that have shaped every individual.

Take, for instance, the somewhat controversial debates surrounding cultural appropriation. While the essence of the concern is valid, it sometimes becomes a tool for division. In our envisioned world, instead of viewing cultural exchanges as potential minefields, they'd be seen as opportunities to celebrate, understand, and respect the rich tapestry of human civilization. A teenager wearing a traditional garment from another culture wouldn't be met with immediate outrage but might be approached with curiosity and an opportunity for dialogue.

The world of mutual respect and understanding also extends beyond inter-human interactions. It encompasses our relationship with nature, animals, and the planet at large. Recognizing that our actions have broader implications and that respect must be universal would be foundational in this envisaged world.

## Steps that Individuals, Communities, and Nations Can Take to Contribute to This Vision

The journey to such an inclusive and understanding world begins at the individual level. Personal introspection and education are crucial. By seeking out diverse narratives, whether through literature, travel, or conversation, individuals can break down deeply ingrained stereotypes and prejudices. One might consider enrolling in cultural exchange programs, attending workshops, or merely engaging in genuine conversations with someone from a different background.

Communities can foster this spirit by organizing multicultural events, promoting arts from various cultures, and providing platforms for marginalized voices. Creating spaces where people can share their stories, and where others can listen, is a potent tool against prejudice and misunderstanding. A community might sponsor events like "Human Libraries," where individuals share personal stories and experiences, allowing attendees to "read" them like open books.

Nations have a monumental role in promoting mutual respect and understanding. This can be achieved through inclusive education curriculums, cultural exchange programs, and diplomatic endeavors that prioritize mutual respect. Policies that discourage divisive rhetoric and promote unity are vital. Consider, for instance, Canada's approach to multiculturalism, which, while not without its challenges, has been a cornerstone of its national identity and seeks to appreciate the diverse cultures that make up its fabric.

## Emphasizing Collective Responsibility and the Power of Individual Actions

The creation of a harmonious society is not the sole responsibility of any one individual or institution; it is a collective endeavor. Every interaction, no matter how small, contributes to the societal fabric. A single act of kindness, understanding, or open-mindedness can have ripple effects, altering perceptions and breaking barriers. Conversely, perpetuating stereotypes or engaging in divisive behavior, even unconsciously, can perpetuate cycles of misunderstanding and prejudice.

An example of the power of individual actions can be seen in the story of Daryl Davis, a black musician who, over the years, befriended numerous members of the Ku Klux Klan. Through genuine dialogue and friendship, many of these individuals eventually left the Klan. Davis's actions underscore the profound impact of individual efforts rooted in understanding and patience.

Collective responsibility reminds us that we're in this together. While institutions, leaders, and policymakers play a pivotal role, the onus is also on every individual to contribute to the vision of a harmonious society. It calls for self-awareness, continued education, and a commitment to approaching the world and its diverse inhabitants with an open heart and mind.

# Chapter 11
# The Absurdity of Overreach and the Question of Responsibility

## *To the Extremes*

**Highlighting and Dissecting the Most Outlandish Examples of PC Overreach**

Over the years, as the wave of political correctness swept across various spheres of life, there have been moments when its implementation bordered on the absurd. These instances, while not representative of the broader movement's goals, have nonetheless caught significant attention due to their sheer extremity. One example, reported in various media outlets, was the controversy surrounding a college in the U.S. where yoga classes were suspended because of concerns over "cultural appropriation." While the intentions were rooted in respect for another culture, the decision failed to recognize that yoga, as a practice, is something that has been willingly shared and spread by those within the culture. To bar individuals from practicing it in the name of "political correctness" seemed counterintuitive.

In another instance, an elementary school reportedly considered removing the classic children's game, "tag," from its playground, citing concerns that it could be too aggressive and might hurt children's feelings. While the school's concerns about emotional well-being are noteworthy, some argue that such steps could stifle natural child play and interactions. These cases highlight the risks of applying blanket solutions without considering nuances and broader implications.

## Discussing the Implications and Consequences of These Extremes on Society

While it might be easy to dismiss these examples as mere anomalies in the broader discourse of political correctness, they bear significant implications. Firstly, such extreme instances can distort the public's perception of the core tenets of political correctness, reducing it to a caricature of its genuine intentions. For those already skeptical of the PC movement, these instances serve as ammunition, perpetuating the narrative that political correctness is nothing more than an overzealous attempt to police behavior and speech.

Moreover, when taken to extremes, PC overreach can inadvertently stifle free expression and creativity. If creators, educators, and the general public constantly second-guess their actions, fearful of offending or overstepping invisible lines, it can lead to a culture of self-censorship. Such a climate might suppress novel ideas, diverse expressions, and innovative thoughts, all in the name of avoiding potential backlash.

Lastly, these extremes can overshadow genuine issues. By focusing on relatively trivial matters, the public's attention might be diverted from pressing, systemic challenges that require attention. When the discourse is dominated by controversies surrounding school games or yoga classes, issues like racial inequality, gender discrimination, or economic disparities might get sidelined.

## How Media Amplification Often Exacerbates and Sensationalizes These Instances

Media, in its pursuit of attention-grabbing headlines and increased viewership, often plays a role in amplifying these extreme instances of PC overreach. Sensational stories are more likely to be shared, discussed, and debated, providing media outlets with higher engagement rates. In a way, the media ecosystem rewards controversy, and stories of extreme political correctness fit neatly into this paradigm.

The issue with this media amplification is that it distorts public perception. Instead of understanding political correctness as a nuanced, multifaceted movement aimed at promoting respect and understanding, it gets reduced to these outlandish episodes. Over time, this can breed resentment and skepticism towards genuine attempts at fostering inclusivity and understanding.

Additionally, this amplification can create a feedback loop. Seeing the attention garnered by extreme instances, individuals and institutions might consciously or subconsciously engage in further overreaches, expecting media coverage or public attention. This perpetuates a cycle where the discourse around political correctness becomes increasingly detached from its foundational principles.

## *The Hyper-Sensitivity Era*

### Tracing the Societal Progression from Awareness to Overt Sensitivity to Perceived Slights

Over the last few decades, there has been a marked shift in societal consciousness. What began as a commendable effort to raise awareness about previously ignored or marginalized issues soon morphed into a heightened state of alertness. Take, for instance, the case of "microaggressions." Initially, this term was introduced to shed light on subtle, often unintentional, discriminatory remarks or actions that minority groups face regularly. However, as the term became mainstream, its application broadened to a point where everyday interactions, innocent comments, or benign gestures were heavily scrutinized, leading to accusations and strained relations.

Another example from the world of literature can be cited. Mark Twain's "Adventures of Huckleberry Finn" faced calls for banning or modification in some schools due to its use of racial slurs. While it's crucial to be sensitive to the damaging effects of derogatory language, critics argue that omitting such words overlooks the historical context and the very essence of the work, which critiques the deeply rooted racism of its time.

Such instances indicate that the pendulum may have swung from benign ignorance to a phase of overt sensitivity, where even well-intentioned actions are viewed with suspicion.

## Discussing the Implications of a Hyper-Aware Society and Its Effect on Discourse and Relationships

A hyper-aware society, while conscious and well-intentioned, may come with unintended consequences. On the one hand, it ensures that marginalized voices are heard and their concerns addressed. On the other hand, it might create an atmosphere of fear and defensiveness, where people are hesitant to voice their opinions or engage in open dialogue. Conversations become minefields, with participants tiptoeing around topics, wary of potential backlash.

Such a state of affairs can hinder authentic relationships. When individuals cannot be their authentic selves for fear of unintentional slights, it can prevent deeper connections based on mutual understanding and vulnerability. Moreover, instead of fostering an environment of learning and growth, where mistakes are viewed as opportunities for enlightenment, a hyper-aware society might penalize even the slightest misstep.

There's also the danger of dilution. When every minor slight or disagreement is amplified to the level of significant transgressions, it may diminish the impact of addressing genuine, systemic issues. The focus shifts from rectifying glaring injustices to nitpicking minor infractions.

## Analyzing Whether Society's Heightened Sensitivity Serves to Unite or Divide

At its heart, the drive towards heightened sensitivity springs from a noble aspiration: to create a more inclusive, understanding, and harmonious society. And indeed, in many instances, this heightened sensitivity has brought to light issues that were previously swept under the rug, giving voice to the voiceless and ensuring a more equitable space for all. However, the extremes of this trend may inadvertently sow seeds of division.

When taken to its extreme, hyper-sensitivity can foster a "call-out culture," where public shaming becomes the norm. Such a culture, while it may deter problematic behavior, can also create deep-seated resentment among those who feel they're walking on eggshells. The fear of public humiliation or the stress of constantly monitoring one's behavior might turn people away from engaging in meaningful dialogues or participating in social causes.

Moreover, while heightened sensitivity aims to bridge divides and promote unity, its extremes can lead to fragmentation. Different groups, wary of the others' perceived hypersensitivities, might choose to self-segregate, leading to echo chambers where only homogeneous thoughts and views are propagated.

In conclusion, while heightened sensitivity has its merits, like most things, balance is key. Without a tempered approach, what aims to unite might ironically end up dividing.

## *Ownership of Emotion*

**Delving into the Psychology of Personal Responsibility in the Face of Offense**

At the heart of the contemporary debate surrounding political correctness lies the psychological concept of personal responsibility, especially in response to perceived offenses. When someone feels offended or hurt by another's words or actions, who bears the onus of that emotional response? Traditional models of emotional intelligence have always stressed the significance of individuals owning their feelings and reactions. It suggests that while external factors can influence our emotional states, the final responsibility for how we feel and, more importantly, how we respond, lies within us. Dr. Albert Ellis, a renowned psychologist and creator of Rational Emotive Behavior Therapy (REBT), argued that our reactions to events are shaped more by our perceptions and beliefs about the events than the events themselves. In the realm of political correctness, this idea would imply that it isn't just the comment or action that causes offense, but the interpretation of that comment by the recipient.

In recent years, however, there's been a shifting perspective. As societal awareness grew regarding marginalized groups and historical grievances, the discourse moved towards a space where the onus of not causing offense was placed squarely on the speaker. While this has the positive effect of making people more considerate and mindful, critics argue that it risks creating a society where individuals are not equipped to handle dissent, disagreement, or unintentional slights, as they never cultivate the emotional resilience to do so.

## Arguing for the Importance of Emotional Autonomy in a Hyper-Sensitive Society

Emotional autonomy, the capacity to be in charge of one's emotional reactions, is pivotal in a society that is rapidly evolving in terms of its understanding of free speech, respect, and sensitivity. The reason being, a society that overemphasizes the avoidance of causing offense might inadvertently cultivate individuals who are externally reactive. In such a setting, one's emotional well-being is perpetually tethered to external stimuli, making them vulnerable and giving undue power to others over their emotional states.

Consider, for instance, the world of academia. There have been instances where guest lecturers were disinvited from universities or faced intense backlash because their topics might upset some students. While the intention—to protect students from potential harm—is commendable, a counterargument arises: Isn't the very essence of education to challenge existing beliefs, introduce new perspectives, and sometimes, make one uncomfortable? By shielding individuals from potentially "harmful" ideas, are we not depriving them of the opportunity to develop emotional autonomy?

Furthermore, having emotional autonomy does not mean one becomes cold or indifferent. Instead, it equips individuals to choose their battles wisely, deciding where their energy and emotional investment should go, and fosters a sense of inner resilience that is invaluable in navigating the complexities of modern society.

**Case Studies Showcasing Positive Outcomes When Individuals Chose to Take Personal Responsibility Over Their Reactions**

One remarkable case study emerges from Daryl Davis, an African-American musician who chose an unconventional approach to confront racism. Instead of reacting with understandable anger and resentment towards members of the Ku Klux Klan, Davis engaged them in dialogue. Over time, his efforts led to over 200 Klan members renouncing their beliefs and giving up their robes. Davis exemplifies how taking personal responsibility over reactions can lead to transformative results. Instead of being a passive recipient of prejudice, he took proactive steps, grounded in emotional autonomy, to address the root of the issue.

Another notable instance can be found in the realm of restorative justice. In New Zealand, a program called "Restorative Circles" brings together offenders and victims to discuss the offense, its implications, and potential ways of reconciliation. Instead of focusing on punishment, the emphasis is on understanding and healing. Many victims, instead of reacting with vengeance, take responsibility for their healing journey by engaging with those who harmed them, leading to profound outcomes for both parties involved.

Lastly, the global phenomenon of "Humans of New York" provides countless anecdotes of individuals from diverse backgrounds who chose to take charge of their stories, emotions, and reactions. From tales of forgiveness after immense betrayal to understanding after grave misunderstandings, these stories underscore the power of emotional autonomy and the magic that unfolds when individuals choose understanding over resentment.

## *Dialogues Over Dictatorship*

### Advocating for Open, Respectful Dialogues as a Remedy for Misunderstandings

The very essence of a vibrant and democratic society lies in its ability to encourage open, respectful dialogues on a myriad of topics, even when they touch upon sensitive or controversial issues. The emphasis on dialogue emerges from an understanding that it's only through communication that misunderstandings can be rectified and knowledge can be enhanced. In contrast, a culture that veers too heavily towards political correctness often runs the risk of shutting down discourse in the fear of causing offense.

For instance, in various universities across the world, there's been a noticeable trend wherein certain speakers or ideas are shut out due to concerns about offending specific groups or individuals. While protection from harm is a valid concern, one might argue that the academic environment, above all, should be a bastion of free thought, even if it's uncomfortable. Encouraging dialogue, even with ideas we vehemently disagree with, fosters critical thinking, discernment, and the ability to counter flawed arguments with logic and reason.

The philosopher Karl Popper once posited the notion of the "open society", a society where individuals are encouraged to think critically, and ideas are open to scrutiny, criticism, and debate. It's a vision that rests on the belief that through the crucible of open dialogue, truth emerges, and society progresses. While political correctness aims to protect, overzealous application might inadvertently stifle the very conversations that lead to understanding and progress.

## Discussing the Societal Cost When Open Communication is Stifled or Repressed

Stifling open communication, especially in the name of political correctness, carries significant societal costs. For starters, it creates a simmering undercurrent of resentment among those who feel their voices are being suppressed. This resentment, when left unaddressed, can manifest in various ways, including an increasing polarization in society. Instead of engaging in constructive dialogue, individuals might retreat to their echo chambers, only interacting with those who share their beliefs and vilifying those who don't.

A prime example of this can be observed in the political landscapes of various countries where extreme polarization has led to a breakdown in civil discourse. Individuals, feeling that their perspectives are not given a legitimate platform, may resort to radical means to make their voices heard or gravitate towards demagogues who exploit these feelings of marginalization.

Furthermore, repressing open dialogue can hinder societal progress. History is replete with examples where challenging the status quo and discussing "taboo" subjects led to significant advancements in human rights, scientific understanding, and societal well-being. By curbing these discussions, society risks stagnation, potentially missing out on transformative ideas and solutions to pressing problems.

## Proposing Methods and Techniques for Fostering Healthy, Constructive Conversations in Diverse Settings

To navigate the fine line between respectful discourse and political correctness, it's vital to introduce methods that promote constructive conversations. One such method is the "Socratic Seminar", an age-old teaching technique where participants seek deeper understanding of complex ideas through rigorously thoughtful dialogue, rather than by memorizing bits of information. By promoting open-ended questions, active listening, and respectful disagreement, this technique could serve as a model for conversations in various settings.

In corporate environments, diversity and inclusion training can play a crucial role. However, instead of simply focusing on what not to say, these programs could emphasize the value of diverse perspectives, teaching employees to engage with curiosity rather than defensiveness. Techniques such as "reflective listening", where participants echo back what they've heard to confirm understanding, can be invaluable.

Finally, in public and online discourse, platforms could employ "structured dialogue" formats, where discussions are carefully facilitated to ensure that all voices are heard and respected. Online forums and social media platforms could integrate tools that prompt users to reflect before posting potentially offensive content or introduce "cooling-off" periods for heated discussions. By prioritizing understanding over winning an argument, society can move towards more constructive and less divisive conversations.

## *Danger of Suppression*

### The Risks Associated with Suppressing Genuine Queries, Doubts, or Debates

The cornerstone of any vibrant society is the free exchange of ideas, a platform where genuine queries, doubts, and debates can be presented without fear of retaliation. However, in the pursuit of avoiding offense, there's a risk of suppressing these genuine expressions. By doing so, society risks stifling innovation, intellectual growth, and even the path to mutual understanding.

Historical precedents provide insight into the dangers of suppression. During the Middle Ages, for instance, the Church often suppressed scientific queries that contradicted religious beliefs, leading to stagnation in various fields of study. Galileo Galilei's persecution for his heliocentric model is a poignant example of this. In modern times, when genuine concerns or debates are brushed aside or labeled as "politically incorrect", it creates a sense of disillusionment and alienation among individuals. They feel that their genuine efforts to understand or engage are being rejected, leading to resentment or apathy.

Moreover, when society suppresses or marginalizes certain voices, it indirectly sends a message that some questions are forbidden or that some doubts are invalid. This environment is antithetical to the tenets of democracy and freedom, and instead of fostering a community of understanding and cooperation, it engenders a climate of distrust and hesitance.

## How Suppression Might Inadvertently Promote Misinformation or Misunderstanding

Suppressing genuine debates and queries has another grave consequence: the inadvertent promotion of misinformation and misunderstanding. When topics become taboo or off-limits for discussion, they don't just disappear; instead, they often move to less regulated, more echo-chamber-like environments where misinformation can thrive unchecked.

For example, when certain health-related queries or doubts are labeled as "misinformation" and suppressed without proper addressal, they find refuge in niche online communities. These platforms often lack proper fact-checking or diverse perspectives. Over time, these misconceptions can become deeply entrenched beliefs for their followers, leading to real-world consequences, such as vaccine hesitancy or alternative medicine over-dependence.

Further, suppression doesn't allow for clarifications, corrections, or enlightenment. If a person has a flawed understanding or a misconception and is immediately shut down when they voice it, they never get the chance to be corrected or educated. They walk away with their misunderstandings intact, perhaps even reinforced by the negative experience of being silenced.

**Strategies for Promoting a Culture that Celebrates Curiosity and Questioning**

One of the foundational steps in fostering a culture of curiosity is emphasizing education. School curriculums should not just focus on rote learning but encourage critical thinking, where students are taught to question, analyze, and derive conclusions based on evidence. The Socratic method, where educators pose questions to stimulate critical thinking, can be particularly effective.

Another strategy is to offer platforms for open debates and dialogues, where individuals from diverse backgrounds come together to discuss pressing issues without the fear of backlash. Universities, community centers, and even online platforms can host such events, ensuring they're moderated to maintain civility and respect.

Lastly, society, as a whole, should work towards creating a culture that values and respects questions. This can be done through public campaigns, literature, and media that celebrate the stories of scientists, activists, and thinkers who've advanced human understanding through their relentless queries and doubts. Instead of shaming or suppressing doubt, society should view it as a steppingstone towards greater knowledge and understanding.

## *The Illusion of Total Agreement*

**Dissecting the Fallacy that Society Can or Should Reach a Consensus on Every Topic**

The idea that a diverse, complex society can reach total agreement on every contentious issue is a lofty one. While cohesion and common values are necessary for a functioning society, expecting unanimity on every topic is not only unrealistic but also potentially counterproductive.

This illusion is often driven by the noble intent of seeking harmony, but in reality, consensus is rarely achieved without some form of coercion, suppression, or oversimplification of nuanced issues.

For instance, consider the intense debates on climate change. While there's a broad scientific consensus on its anthropogenic causes and impacts, how each country should tackle it, the role of businesses versus governments, and the priorities set in addressing it can vary vastly. Assuming that there can be a singular, universally accepted solution might oversimplify the intricate dynamics of this global challenge.

Moreover, the push for total agreement can inadvertently stifle free speech and hinder the free exchange of ideas. For example, in certain academic settings, there have been concerns that the fear of offending has led to self-censorship among scholars, affecting the quality and breadth of academic discourse. By holding consensus as the gold standard, society risks silencing minority voices or unpopular opinions that might offer valuable insights or critiques.

## Emphasizing the Value of Diversity in Thought and Belief

Diversity in thought and belief is not just inevitable in a free society; it's invaluable. Different perspectives, born out of varying life experiences, cultures, and educations, enrich debates, and often lead to more comprehensive solutions. The marketplace of ideas, a principle advocating for freedom of expression within a democratic society, operates under the belief that the truth emerges from the competition of ideas in free, transparent public discourse.

For instance, the civil rights movement in the U.S., which profoundly changed societal norms and laws, was born out of dissenting voices challenging the status quo. If society had clung to a false consensus and suppressed these voices, transformative changes would not have been realized.

Additionally, it's worth noting that conformity in thought can lead to stagnation. History is replete with examples of societies that flourished when they embraced diversity—be it the Islamic Golden Age where scholars of different faiths collaborated, or the Renaissance, which thrived on a mix of ideas from different cultures and epochs.

**Strategies for Coexistence in a Pluralistic Society**

The key to coexistence in a pluralistic society lies not in enforced consensus but in mutual respect and understanding. First and foremost, education systems should place emphasis on teaching critical thinking, empathy, and active listening. By understanding and valuing different perspectives, even if one doesn't agree with them, individuals can engage in more constructive dialogues.

Secondly, media platforms and public forums should champion diverse voices. Instead of echo chambers that reinforce pre-existing beliefs, platforms should curate content that challenges and broadens perspectives. This not only informs the public but also fosters tolerance for differing viewpoints.

Lastly, legal and societal frameworks should protect freedom of expression while also ensuring that this freedom is not used to incite violence or discrimination. Laws that strike a balance between upholding free speech and penalizing "hate" speech, coupled with public campaigns promoting unity in diversity, can guide societies towards harmonious coexistence. Through these measures, societies can celebrate plurality without descending into discord.

## *Strategies for Navigating PC Overreach*

**Practical Tips and Solutions for Individuals and Communities to Manage Overzealous PC Norms**

In an age where a misplaced word or an inadvertent gesture can lead to public outcry, individuals and communities often find themselves walking on eggshells, attempting to conform to ever-shifting standards of political correctness. It's essential, therefore, to equip oneself with tools to navigate this complex terrain.

Firstly, maintaining open channels of communication is pivotal. When in doubt, ask. It's better to seek clarity on potentially sensitive topics than to make assumptions, which often lead to misunderstandings. For example, in multicultural workspaces, fostering a culture where employees feel comfortable asking about unfamiliar cultural norms can prevent unintentional offenses.

Secondly, one can take a proactive approach by educating oneself on current societal norms and expectations. This doesn't mean one has to agree or conform to all of them, but awareness can help individuals make informed decisions. Community workshops or seminars on topics related to inclusivity, sensitivity, and communication can be beneficial in this regard.

Lastly, it's essential to understand the distinction between intent and impact. While one's intentions might be pure, the impact of one's actions might differ. In cases of unintended harm, owning up, apologizing, and learning from the experience is a constructive way forward, rather than becoming defensive.

## Fostering Self-awareness and Critical Thinking in the Face of External Pressures

While societal norms exert pressure on individuals to conform, it's crucial to cultivate an internal compass grounded in self-awareness and critical thinking. This means continually reflecting on one's beliefs, biases, and actions, ensuring they align with one's core values rather than external pressures.

For example, the cancel culture phenomenon can sometimes lead to a rush to judgment without fully understanding context or intent. In such cases, before joining the fray, one might pause to gather comprehensive information, critically analyze the situation, and then form an opinion. This not only protects against being swept up in potentially misinformed mob mentality but also promotes a more nuanced and informed perspective.

Encouraging platforms like debate clubs, reading groups, or community discussions that emphasize critical thinking can help individuals strengthen this skill. These platforms can challenge participants to think deeply about issues, consider diverse viewpoints, and articulate their positions cogently.

**Encouraging Resilience and Adaptability in an Ever-evolving Societal Landscape**

Change is the only constant in our societal landscape, especially in our fast-paced, globalized world. With the rapid evolution of norms and values, resilience and adaptability become invaluable traits. Instead of feeling threatened or overwhelmed by change, one can view it as an opportunity for growth and learning.

One way to foster resilience is to focus on one's core values and principles. While societal norms might shift, having a strong internal foundation provides stability and direction. For instance, if one values respect and understanding, this can guide interactions even in unfamiliar situations, ensuring one remains true to oneself while adapting to new scenarios.

Furthermore, adaptability involves recognizing that one's understanding and perspectives will continuously evolve. It's okay to change one's mind or to learn new things. The key is to remain open-minded and curious. For instance, attending workshops or courses on emerging societal issues, or engaging with diverse groups to understand varied perspectives, can enhance adaptability.

In conclusion, while the challenges posed by overzealous political correctness can seem daunting, with self-awareness, critical thinking, resilience, and adaptability, individuals and communities can navigate this terrain with confidence and integrity.

# Chapter 12
# The Dual Sides of Respect:
# Navigating the Personal and Societal

## *The Pivotal Chapter*

**Explaining Why Understanding Respect, Both Personal and Societal, is Foundational in Eliminating the Need for Political Correctness**

At its core, the emergence of political correctness was rooted in a noble aspiration: to foster respect and consideration for all, irrespective of their backgrounds, beliefs, and identities. However, as we've seen throughout this book, the execution of this ideal has not always been flawless, sometimes leading to overreaches that stifle expression and promote conformity over genuine understanding. If we peel back the layers of the PC phenomenon, we find that understanding and practicing genuine respect—both personal and societal—is the key to addressing many of its pitfalls.

From a personal perspective, respect goes beyond just using the "right" terms or avoiding certain phrases. It requires a deeper recognition of the intrinsic worth of every individual, seeing them beyond labels or stereotypes. For instance, while it might be politically correct to avoid certain terms that might be deemed derogatory, genuine personal respect would involve understanding the person's experiences, listening to their stories, and empathizing with their challenges.

Societal respect, on the other hand, involves creating an environment where all members feel valued and heard. This goes beyond just setting rules about what can or cannot be said. Instead, it looks at creating structures and systems that provide equal opportunities, dismantle systemic biases, and champion diversity in all its forms. For instance, instead of just teaching about the harms of racial slurs, societal respect would involve creating curricula that highlight the contributions of various racial and ethnic groups, debunking racial myths, and promoting intercultural understanding.

**Introducing the Overarching Themes and Narratives of the Chapter**

As we delve deeper into this chapter, our journey will revolve around several key themes. Firstly, we will explore the nuanced differences between personal and societal respect. While interconnected, these two facets of respect play distinct roles in shaping our interactions and societal structures. For example, personal respect might dictate our one-on-one interactions, while societal respect shapes policies, media representation, and public discourses.

Secondly, we'll tackle the limitations of political correctness in promoting genuine respect. While PC norms can provide a framework, they often only address the surface-level manifestations of disrespect, neglecting deeper systemic issues or personal biases. For instance, a company might enforce a strict PC language policy but still harbor a toxic work culture where microaggressions or subtle biases are rampant.

Lastly, we will consider how individuals, communities, and institutions can move beyond mere political correctness towards a more holistic understanding and practice of respect. This involves looking beyond rules and guidelines and fostering an ethos of empathy, understanding, and mutual appreciation. As a case in point, consider a school that doesn't just implement anti-bullying rules but actively promotes empathy training, conflict resolution skills, and intergroup dialogues, ensuring students internalize the value of respect.

In essence, this chapter will challenge readers to rethink their understanding of respect, highlighting its transformative potential in creating a world where the genuine appreciation of diversity eliminates the need for surface-level PC protocols.

## *Personal Boundaries vs. Societal Norms*

**Dissecting the Tension between Individual Feelings and Broad Societal Expectations**

The dance between individual autonomy and societal compliance is an age-old tension, intensified in the era of political correctness. Personal boundaries are the individual's self-set rules or limits, which define what is permissible behavior towards them. They are unique to every individual, shaped by a myriad of factors including upbringing, cultural background, personal experiences, and innate disposition. On the other side of the coin, societal norms are the unspoken and formal rules and expectations set by a larger community or culture, directing how its members should behave, speak, or interact.

For instance, let's consider a university setting. A student from a conservative background might have personal boundaries against using profanity or engaging in certain conversations. Meanwhile, the broader university culture, influenced by a mixture of diverse backgrounds and progressive ideals, might have a more relaxed attitude towards these subjects. When these two worlds collide, the student may feel out of place, misunderstood, or pressured to conform.

**Exploring the Consequences When Personal Boundaries Clash with Collective Norms**

When personal boundaries are at odds with societal norms, the outcomes can be complex and multifaceted. For individuals, it might result in feelings of alienation, stress, or identity crises. They may constantly feel like outsiders, perpetually battling to defend their personal boundaries against a seemingly monolithic societal force. An example could be drawn from religious individuals in largely secular societies. For instance, a devout Muslim woman choosing to wear a hijab might find herself facing discrimination or misunderstandings in Western countries where the headscarf has been misinterpreted or is not a societal norm.

However, it's not just individuals who bear the brunt of these clashes. Societies also stand to lose. A society that cannot accommodate diverse personal boundaries risks homogenization, stifling creativity, and can breed resentment among its members. There might be instances where, in the name of political correctness, individuals are chastised for their deeply held beliefs, causing them to become more insular and less trusting of the larger community.

## Strategies for Achieving Balance and Harmony

Achieving a balance between personal boundaries and societal norms, especially in the landscape of political correctness, requires a multifaceted approach.

Firstly, education plays a pivotal role. Through education, individuals can be made aware of the diverse tapestry of beliefs, lifestyles, and personal boundaries that exist within their community. This awareness can foster mutual respect and understanding. Schools, for instance, can incorporate courses that focus on world religions, diverse cultural practices, and even seminars on personal boundaries, making students more empathetic and aware.

Secondly, creating platforms for dialogue is essential. Community town halls, interfaith dialogues, or cultural exchange programs can be instrumental in bridging gaps. Here, instead of stifling discussions in the name of political correctness, diverse opinions are aired, understood, and respected.

Lastly, it's crucial for societies to regularly re-evaluate and evolve their norms. Societal norms shouldn't be static but should adapt to the changing demographics and beliefs of its members. As society grows more diverse, norms should be inclusive and accommodating, allowing for a harmonious coexistence of multiple personal boundaries without any group feeling marginalized or suppressed.

<h1 style="text-align:center">Our Inherent Biases</h1>

## A Deep Dive into the Psychology of Biases and How They Shape Our Views on Respect

Human cognition is a product of both evolution and personal experiences. Throughout history, our ancestors had to quickly assess their surroundings for potential threats, leading to the development of certain cognitive shortcuts or biases. These biases, while once crucial for survival, often operate in the background, influencing our judgments and decisions in a myriad of contexts, including our views on respect.

For example, consider the "confirmation bias," where individuals tend to seek, interpret, and remember information that confirms their pre-existing beliefs. In the realm of political correctness, this bias might manifest when an individual only acknowledges instances that further their belief that PC culture is either inherently good or bad, while disregarding evidence to the contrary. This tunnel vision, reinforced by biases, can distort one's view on respect, making them believe that their version of respect (or lack thereof) is universally applicable or acceptable.

## The Interplay of Culture, Upbringing, and Experiences in Shaping These Biases

While our evolutionary history laid the foundation for biases, they're further molded by our personal experiences, cultural background, and upbringing. These factors collectively act as the lens through which we view the world. Our early years, especially, play a pivotal role in cementing certain biases. For instance, if one grows up in a homogenous community with little exposure to diversity, they might unconsciously develop biases against unfamiliar cultures or practices.

A classic example would be the case of sushi. In many Western countries, the initial response to sushi (raw fish) was one of disgust or apprehension, often stemming from cultural biases that equated raw food with being unclean or dangerous. Yet, as globalization increased exposure to Japanese culture and cuisine, these biases were challenged, leading to sushi's now widespread popularity. Similarly, in the context of respect, our inherent biases can make us resistant to forms of respect or expressions that don't align with what we're familiar with, thereby coloring our interactions with those from different backgrounds.

## How Recognizing and Challenging Biases Can Lead to More Inclusive Perspectives

Awareness is the first step towards change. Recognizing that biases are innate and universal, rather than a personal failing, can make individuals more open to addressing them. Cognitive biases, much like habits, can be altered or replaced once recognized. This involves continuously challenging one's beliefs, seeking diverse experiences, and intentionally placing oneself in situations that contradict one's biases.

Taking workshops on unconscious biases or engaging in open dialogues about controversial topics can be illuminating. Such environments force individuals to re-evaluate their deeply-held beliefs in the light of new information. Furthermore, cultivating empathy by immersing oneself in diverse cultural settings or reading literature from varied perspectives can pave the way for a broader, more inclusive understanding of respect.

In the end, in a world striving for true respect and understanding, unearthing, and grappling with our biases isn't just beneficial—it's essential. By challenging our biases, we not only enrich our own perspectives but also pave the way for a society that's truly respectful and inclusive, beyond the superficial layers of political correctness.

## *The Balance Beam of Sensitivity*

## Outlining the Challenges of Promoting Respect Without Compromising Free Expression

Promoting respect in diverse settings often feels like walking a tightrope. On one end of this rope is the pursuit of a society where everyone feels respected, valued, and protected from harmful behaviors or expressions. On the other end lies the sanctity of free speech, an integral tenet in democratic societies that assures individuals the liberty to express their beliefs, however controversial or unconventional they may be. Balancing these two values is a herculean challenge. Push too hard for unrestricted expression, and it might allow for hate speech or harmful rhetoric to thrive. Overemphasize sensitivity, and you run the risk of creating an environment where individuals fear speaking out, lest they be labeled as offensive.

For instance, university campuses, traditionally bastions of free thought and debate, have sometimes been critiqued for their alleged stifling of certain views in the name of creating "safe spaces". While the intent — to protect marginalized or vulnerable students — is commendable, critics argue that it sometimes veers into the territory of censoring unpopular or dissenting voices, thereby stifling genuine dialogue and debate.

## Emphasizing the Adage "Respect is Earned, Not Given" and Its Implications in a PC World

The phrase "respect is earned, not given" is often invoked to emphasize the notion that respect should be a two-way street, based on mutual understanding and recognition. In an ideal world, every individual would strive to earn respect through their actions, words, and integrity. However, the growing emphasis on political correctness sometimes shifts the focus from genuine, earned respect to a mandated, superficial courtesy.

Let's consider the workplace as an example. In a bid to be politically correct, a company might mandate employees to use specific language or adopt certain behaviors. While these guidelines might prevent overt offenses, they could also inadvertently promote an environment where employees simply comply out of obligation, rather than genuine understanding or empathy. The result? A workplace that's politically correct on the surface, but potentially lacks the deeper, more meaningful respect that comes from genuine mutual understanding and appreciation.

**Strategies for Fostering Genuine Respect in Diverse Settings**

Achieving genuine respect in diverse environments, be it a workplace, a school, or a community, is no small feat. However, there are actionable strategies that can be implemented to encourage authentic respect:

1. **Education and Exposure**: Organize workshops, seminars, and training sessions that delve into various cultures, traditions, and experiences. Exposure to diverse perspectives can foster empathy and genuine respect.

2. **Encourage Open Dialogues**: Create platforms where individuals can freely express their viewpoints, ask questions, and engage in constructive debates. These platforms should be safe spaces where no question is "off-limits", fostering an environment where individuals learn from each other.

3. **Promote Critical Thinking**: Encourage individuals to challenge their biases, assumptions, and preconceived notions. Rather than simply adhering to a set of PC guidelines, individuals should be equipped to think critically about their beliefs and behaviors.

Ultimately, genuine respect stems from understanding and empathy, which can't be mandated or enforced. By focusing on education, open dialogues, and critical thinking, we can hope to cultivate an environment where respect is indeed earned and given in equal measure.

## *From PC to Mutual Respect*

**Arguing for a Shift from Strict Political Correctness to Genuine, Mutual Respect**

The rise of political correctness, initially, was to ensure marginalized and underrepresented groups felt safe, heard, and respected. Over time, however, the emphasis on adhering to PC standards has sometimes overshadowed the core principle behind its inception: mutual respect. When people begin to prioritize the avoidance of certain words or phrases merely to fit into a socially accepted mold, without a genuine understanding of the rationale behind it, the result is superficial conformity rather than authentic respect.

Imagine, for instance, attending a multicultural festival. While the surface may be adorned with colors, music, and food from various cultures, if attendees only engage with these elements superficially— taking pictures for social media, sampling food without understanding its origins or significance—the event becomes an aesthetic experience devoid of genuine respect for the cultures represented. Similarly, an environment that strictly adheres to PC norms without understanding or appreciating the reasons behind them is one that misses the mark.

**Presenting Case Studies that Showcase the Transformative Power of Mutual Respect over Imposed PC Norms**

### Case Study 1: A University Classroom Setting

At a renowned university, a professor, aiming to foster an inclusive environment, established a strict set of guidelines emphasizing political correctness. Initially, the classroom operated smoothly, with students careful about their choice of words. However, it soon became evident that the emphasis on PC language was stifling genuine dialogue. Instead of understanding and appreciating diverse perspectives, students were fearful of saying the wrong thing and facing potential backlash.

Realizing this, the professor shifted his approach. He encouraged students to share their backgrounds, experiences, and beliefs openly, emphasizing mutual respect and understanding. The results were transformative. Students began engaging in open, sometimes challenging, discussions, but always grounded in a foundation of mutual respect. The environment shifted from one of fear and restriction to one of growth and understanding.

**Case Study 2: A Corporate Office**

A multinational company, in a bid to be inclusive, introduced strict PC guidelines. However, rather than fostering inclusivity, these rules created a sense of alienation among employees. They felt that while the company emphasized certain buzzwords and phrases, there was no genuine effort to understand and cater to the diverse needs of its employees.

Recognizing the growing discontent, the company decided to focus on mutual respect. They organized team-building activities that allowed employees to share personal stories and experiences, workshops that celebrated diversity, and feedback sessions that addressed concerns directly. This shift towards genuine respect and understanding transformed the workplace atmosphere, leading to higher employee satisfaction and improved team dynamics.

**Strategies for Building Societies Founded on Mutual Respect and Understanding**

1. **Promote Empathy**: Organizing workshops or community gatherings that focus on shared human experiences can foster genuine empathy. When individuals understand the struggles, triumphs, and stories of others, they are more likely to approach them with respect.

2. **Encourage Constructive Feedback**: Rather than stifling dialogue, promote environments where individuals can provide constructive feedback. This allows for the rectification of unintentional slights and fosters an environment of continuous learning.

3. **Celebrate Diversity**: Beyond superficial acknowledgments, delve deep into the histories, achievements, and challenges faced by diverse groups. Celebrating diversity in an informed, genuine manner is the cornerstone of mutual respect.

In conclusion, while political correctness serves as a necessary guideline in many scenarios, the ultimate goal should be the cultivation of societies where individuals interact based on mutual respect and understanding, not just adherence to a set of rules.

## *The Pitfalls of Subjective Universalism*

### Examining the Dangers When Every Individual's Unique Beliefs Demand Universal Acknowledgment

Subjective universalism, at its core, revolves around the idea that each individual's unique beliefs, values, and experiences should be universally recognized and acknowledged. While, in theory, it's rooted in a noble desire for inclusivity and acknowledgment of diversity, in practical terms, it can open a Pandora's box of complications. The most apparent danger is the potential for a cacophony of voices, each demanding its unique form of recognition, which could drown out meaningful dialogue and make consensus nearly impossible.

For instance, consider a situation at a multicultural event where every individual participant insists on having their personal customs, no matter how niche, be at the forefront of the event. Instead of leading to greater inclusivity, this could cause disputes over which customs take precedence or garner more attention, overshadowing the very intent of the event. Similarly, if every individual's unique beliefs are placed on the same pedestal without a discerning lens, society might end up acknowledging and potentially even normalizing beliefs that are harmful or regressive.

### Discussing the Practical Impossibilities and Societal Implications of Catering to Every Subjective Belief

The very nature of individual beliefs is that they are subjective and deeply personal. Trying to create a society where every single one of these beliefs is universally acknowledged is not only impractical but could be detrimental. For one, it would demand a constant and infinite expansion of rules, guidelines, and norms to cater to each new subjective belief that emerges.

Imagine a school system trying to implement policies that cater to the diverse and potentially conflicting needs of every single student, teacher, and parent. The administrative nightmare aside, it would also be a breeding ground for constant disagreements, as what may be deemed essential and respectful to one person could be seen as overreach or even disrespect to another.

Beyond practical considerations, the societal implications are profound. If every individual's unique perspective demands universal acknowledgment, it could lead to fragmentation, where people cluster only with those who share their narrow set of beliefs, undermining the very idea of a diverse, integrated society. This hyper-fragmentation can erode shared societal values and foster divisiveness.

## Advocating for Shared Values and Universal Principles as a Unifying Force

As opposed to trying to cater to the vast universe of individual beliefs, a more practical and cohesive approach is to advocate for shared values and universal principles. Such principles provide a common ground upon which diverse societies can stand, fostering unity while still acknowledging diversity.

For instance, principles like human dignity, freedom of expression, and mutual respect are universal enough to be widely accepted yet offer a framework within which diverse beliefs can coexist harmoniously. History offers ample evidence of this: the Universal Declaration of Human Rights, adopted by the United Nations in 1948, is one such document that, while respecting the diverse cultures and histories of the world, lays down certain inalienable rights that every human being is entitled to.

In conclusion, while the intention behind subjective universalism—of acknowledging and respecting every individual's unique beliefs—is commendable, its practical implications can be counterproductive. Instead, focusing on shared values and universal principles provides a more stable and unifying foundation for diverse societies.

## *Introspection: The First Step to Understanding*

### Encouraging Readers to Embark on a Journey of Self-awareness and Self-reflection

In the noise of a society that is increasingly polarized and driven by political correctness, one of the most radical and empowering acts a person can engage in is introspection. It is through turning inwards and examining our beliefs, biases, and behaviors that we begin to truly understand not only ourselves but also the world around us. Introspection is not a retreat from society but rather a deep dive into the inner workings of our mind, enabling us to engage with society more authentically and responsibly.

The adverse effects of political correctness often stem from an external locus of control, where individuals let societal norms dictate their beliefs and actions. This can lead to a disconnect, where individuals may feel constrained or inauthentic in their expressions. For instance, a person might find themselves defending a viewpoint merely because it aligns with a politically correct stance, even if they haven't deeply considered or internalized that viewpoint. Through introspection, one can uncover such inconsistencies and move towards a more congruent self.

### Highlighting the Transformative Power of Introspection in Building Bridges of Happiness and Understanding Ourselves

The transformative power of introspection lies in its ability to liberate us from unconscious biases and unexamined beliefs that can drive divisive behaviors. By actively engaging with our inner thoughts and feelings, we can begin to discern between what we genuinely believe and what has been superimposed upon us by society.

Take the example of Mark, a middle-aged man who grew up in a conservative setting. Due to the environment he was raised in, Mark held certain reservations about gay communities. However, upon introspection, he realized that these views weren't truly his own but were a byproduct of his upbringing. This revelation was transformative, allowing him to unlearn biases and build bridges of understanding with those he had previously distanced himself from.

Furthermore, introspection paves the way for personal happiness. By understanding our desires, fears, and triggers, we become better equipped to navigate the challenges of life, develop resilience, and cultivate inner peace. This deep sense of self-awareness can help individuals navigate the minefields of political correctness with authenticity and grace, rather than fear and defensiveness.

## Offering Tools, Techniques, and Exercises to Promote Self-awareness and Personal Growth

While the journey of introspection is deeply personal, certain tools and techniques can facilitate this process. One such technique is journaling. Regularly writing down one's thoughts, feelings, and experiences can provide clarity and help in recognizing patterns in behavior and belief. For those skeptical about the benefits of journaling, there's an experiment they can try: for one week, dedicate just 10 minutes a day to jot down any strong feelings or reactions to societal events, especially those tied to political correctness. At the end of the week, reading back can often provide insights into deeply ingrained beliefs or biases.

Meditation and mindfulness exercises can also be instrumental in promoting self-awareness. By quieting the mind and focusing on the present moment, individuals can become more attuned to their innermost thoughts and feelings. For beginners, guided meditations, available in abundance online, can be a helpful starting point.

Lastly, engaging in constructive dialogues with diverse groups can be enlightening. By stepping out of one's echo chamber and actively listening to diverse viewpoints, individuals can confront their biases and expand their horizons. Such dialogues, when approached with an open mind, can be as much an exercise in introspection as they are in understanding others.

In conclusion, introspection is a potent antidote to the pitfalls of unexamined political correctness. By delving deep into our psyche, we can move from reactive stances to proactive understanding, laying the foundation for genuine respect and mutual recognition in society.

# Chapter 13
# LGBTQ+ and the Bounds
# of Political Correctness

## *The Precarious Balance of LGBTQ+ Advocacy:*

**Demonstrating cases where LGBTQ+ advocacy is perceived as having gone beyond its genuine cause:**

In the contemporary landscape of LGBTQ+ advocacy, there have been instances where the fervor to champion rights and inclusion appears to have surpassed its original intent. One such case that stirred significant debate was the introduction of a multitude of gender pronouns in educational institutions. While the purpose was to be inclusive of all gender identities, critics argue that it created an environment of undue complexity, with some claiming it bordered on linguistic coercion. A similar sentiment was echoed when businesses started to include exhaustive dropdown menus of gender identities for basic services or sign-ups. For many, while the initial motive of recognizing non-binary and transgender identities was laudable, its implementation felt more like virtue signaling than a sincere effort at inclusion.

**Analyzing the potential backlash and societal division arising from perceived undue privilege to specific groups:**

The risk of societal backlash grows when certain advocacy measures are perceived as granting special privileges rather than rectifying systemic discrimination. One illustration of this is when LGBTQ+ events or parades receive significant city funding or exclusive rights to public spaces, while other community events might not. Detractors argue that such overt favoritism breeds resentment and deepens societal divisions, painting the LGBTQ+ community as receiving preferential treatment. Another contentious issue is when certain LGBTQ+ groups demand that religious institutions change their long-standing doctrines to accommodate modern gender understandings. Critics believe this not only infringes on religious freedoms but also amplifies the "us versus them" dynamic.

**Discussing how such over-extensions might backfire on the broader objectives of the LGBTQ+ movement:**

The broader objective of the LGBTQ+ movement, at its core, is to ensure equality, acceptance, and the eradication of discrimination based on sexual orientation or gender identity. However, when advocacy is perceived as overstepping or demanding special privileges, it can inadvertently hamper the very goals it seeks to achieve. For instance, when LGBTQ+ advocates aggressively challenge traditional community values or institutions, it can foster defensiveness and hinder genuine dialogue. Instead of being perceived as a movement aiming for equal rights, it might be seen as an aggressive force trying to impose its values on others. This perception can alienate potential allies, limit collaborative efforts, and potentially galvanize opposition against LGBTQ+ rights.

## *Transgender Influence and its Perceived Harm on the Young:*

**Detailing instances where transgender teachers and educators are believed to have unduly influenced young minds regarding gender choices:**

There's a growing concern among certain sections of society that the presence of transgender teachers and educators might unduly influence young minds. Some parents and groups argue that having transgender individuals in positions of influence exposes children to perspectives on gender fluidity at an age when they might not have the maturity to fully understand or critically engage with these concepts. For instance, there was notable controversy in the U.S. when a teacher read the book "I Am Jazz", which details the life of a young transgender girl, to a class without notifying parents in advance. Critics argued that discussing transgender topics without parental consent was an overreach, potentially confusing or influencing students. While educators defend such actions as creating inclusive environments, opponents believe it bypasses parents' rights and could prematurely lead children to question their own gender identity.

**Investigating claims of transgender advocacy groups promoting hormone treatments and surgeries for minors:**

Another significant point of contention is the assertion that certain transgender advocacy groups actively promote hormone treatments and surgeries for minors. Critics argue that these medical interventions, which have long-term physical consequences, are being pushed onto young individuals who might not be in a position to make fully informed decisions about their bodies. For instance, in the UK, there was significant scrutiny surrounding the Tavistock clinic's practices. A court case brought forward by a detransitioned individual claimed that the clinic was too quick to prescribe hormone blockers to those under 18. The case reignited debates about the age at which individuals should be allowed to make such life-altering decisions and whether certain advocacy groups might be pushing an aggressive agenda at the expense of vulnerable youths.

**Discussing concerns about the long-term psychological, social, and medical implications for children exposed to aggressive transgender advocacy:**

The repercussions of aggressive transgender advocacy on children are multi-faceted. From a psychological perspective, critics contend that prematurely exposing children to concepts of gender fluidity might lead to unnecessary confusion or distress. There's the fear that children, in their quest to fit in or be seen as unique, might misconstrue temporary feelings of gender dysphoria. On the social front, children expressing desires to transition might face bullying, isolation, or familial disputes, leading to mental health issues. Medically, the use of hormone blockers in prepubescent children is controversial. While some studies indicate they can be safely used to delay puberty, others suggest potential long-term side effects on bone health, fertility, and mental well-being. The overarching concern is whether, in the zeal to support and validate transgender youths, society might inadvertently be paving the way for long-term harm.

## *Dissecting Gender: Biology versus Identity:*

**Delving into the complexities of defining gender purely from a biological standpoint:**

Historically, gender was often viewed through a simplistic lens: a binary derived from biological sex—male or female. This biological standpoint predominantly relied on physical markers like chromosomes, reproductive organs, and hormones. For many, this concrete, anatomical approach is clear and indisputable. They argue that nature itself offers a binary system, evident in the reproductive roles of both sexes. This perspective often gets bolstered by certain religious and cultural teachings which affirm traditional gender roles and definitions. Moreover, a section of the scientific community asserts that the differentiation of roles between males and females, observable even in many animal species, serves evolutionary and reproductive purposes. While biology does present undeniable differences between male and female bodies, the contention arises when these physical attributes are used as the sole determinants to define and restrict gender roles and identities in complex human societies.

**Highlighting the skepticism surrounding the assertion of multiple genders beyond the biological male and female:**

With the rise of gender theory and more nuanced understandings of identity, the concept of gender has expanded beyond strict biological parameters to encompass a spectrum of identities. However, this shift hasn't been without its detractors. Skeptics question the validity of recognizing multiple genders beyond the biologically evident male and female. They argue that by entertaining countless gender identities, society might be venturing into a realm of subjectivity that could have unforeseeable consequences. An example of this skepticism can be seen in the debates around non-binary or gender-neutral pronouns. Critics argue that incorporating such pronouns into everyday language muddles communication and defies grammatical norms, while others believe it forces society to indulge in individual subjectivities. The crux of this skepticism often revolves around the question: Should personal feelings and identities dictate societal norms, especially when they appear to contradict observable biology?

**Understanding the implications of these views on transgender and non-binary communities:**

The debates around gender, particularly when they lean heavily on biological determinism, have profound implications for transgender and non-binary individuals. For many within these communities, their lived experiences often stand in direct contradiction to the binary narrative of gender. Critics, by denying the legitimacy of transgender and non-binary identities, can inadvertently (or sometimes purposefully) invalidate and erase these individuals' experiences. This can lead to feelings of alienation, psychological distress, and societal marginalization for many transgender and non-binary people. For instance, when policies or discourses negate the rights of transgender individuals to access bathrooms aligning with their gender identity, it's not just a matter of logistics or safety but an outright denial of their gender identity. This ongoing tug-of-war between biological definitions of gender and individual gender identities underscores a deep societal rift, with the transgender and non-binary communities often bearing the brunt of the ensuing controversies.


### *Inclusivity or Misplaced Enthusiasm?:*

**Examining the media's zealousness to include LGBTQ+ narratives and how it borders on pandering:**

Over the past decade, media representation of the LGBTQ+ community has skyrocketed. From blockbuster movies to mainstream television series, characters that identify as LGBTQ+ have become increasingly common. While on the surface this seems like a victory for representation, there is a growing argument that this sudden influx borders on pandering. Critics argue that media conglomerates, driven by the desire to appeal to larger demographics and showcase "wokeness," have started to weave in LGBTQ+ characters and narratives not out of genuine advocacy or artistic intent but as a marketing strategy. This approach, they say, commodifies the LGBTQ+ experience, reducing it to a mere trope or plot device rather than a genuine exploration of the community's intricacies. For instance, the phenomenon of "queerbaiting" – where shows or films hint at an LGBTQ+ relationship without ever truly developing it – has been called out as a method to attract LGBTQ+ viewers without actually providing representation.

**Discussing instances where LBGTQ+ characters are in every TV show and movie whereas in real life, most people do not have an LGBTQ+ friend in their lives:**

Another point of contention is the perceived ubiquity of LGBTQ+ characters in media as contrasted with reality. Statistically, while there's a significant portion of the population that identifies as LGBTQ+, their representation in media sometimes seems disproportionately high. Critics often point out that almost every new TV show or movie feels compelled to have an LGBTQ+ character or subplot, creating a skewed perception, especially for younger viewers. They argue that while it's essential for everyone to see themselves represented, the current media landscape might give the impression that LGBTQ+ relationships and experiences are more common than they are in reality. Such a disparity can lead to misconceptions. For example, someone growing up in a predominantly conservative area, with limited exposure to diverse communities in real life, might base their entire understanding of LGBTQ+ dynamics on what they see on screen, which might not always be an accurate or comprehensive depiction.

**Assessing the potential harm of such portrayals in showcasing an overabundance of diversity:**

The implications of this perceived overrepresentation are manifold. Firstly, there's the risk of homogenizing the LGBTQ+ experience. When media repeatedly showcases similar LGBTQ+ narratives or characters that adhere to certain stereotypes – be it the sassy gay friend or the tragic LGBTQ+ storyline – it perpetuates limited views of a diverse community. This can inadvertently rob the community of its varied voices, narratives, and challenges. Secondly, it could lead to backlash. Those skeptical of the LGBTQ+ movement might see this as media propaganda, further entrenching their resistance. There's also the issue of authenticity. The LGBTQ+ community itself sometimes critiques media portrayals as superficial, arguing that while having an LGBTQ+ character is commendable, it's equally important to ensure that their narratives are grounded in real experiences and not just included to tick a representation box. In essence, while increased representation is laudable, it's essential to strike a balance to ensure it doesn't veer into the realm of tokenism or misrepresentation.

## *Navigating the Maze of Personal Identities:*

**Presenting viewpoints that challenge the need for a myriad of individual gender identities:**

As societies have evolved, there's been a significant increase in the recognition of non-traditional gender identities. From non-binary to genderqueer, the spectrum seems to be expanding continually. While many argue that this is a manifestation of societies becoming more inclusive and accepting, others contend that this increasing granularity might be excessive. Some critics posit that the proliferation of gender identities goes beyond the genuine needs of the community and delves into the realm of individualism run amok. They believe that every nuanced personal experience doesn't necessarily warrant its own category or label. For example, while "genderfluid" might resonate as an authentic identity for many, skeptics might ask if it's truly distinct from "non-binary" or if such minute distinctions are necessary. The underlying concern here is that an overemphasis on labels could reduce the potency of the broader LGBTQ+ movement by making it appear fragmented or overly indulgent.

**Discussing potential administrative and societal complications in acknowledging and catering to an expansive list of identities:**

Beyond the realm of socio-political debates, there are practical considerations to take into account. As institutions try to accommodate an expanding list of gender identities, they often find themselves navigating a logistical maze. For instance, universities and public institutions looking to include a range of gender options in official documents might struggle with how exhaustive their lists should be. There's also the matter of spaces like restrooms or dormitories and how to ensure inclusivity without causing undue complications. A school might wonder if they need to have restrooms for ten different gender identities or if a more generalized solution would be more practical. Societal complications arise, too. For example, during group activities or community gatherings, organizers might struggle with addressing or categorizing a diverse array of gender identities. Critics argue that such administrative challenges, while seeming trivial on the surface, could lead to broader inefficiencies and even unintentional exclusions.

**Debating whether an overemphasis on personal identity might detract from broader LGBTQ+ goals:**

The LGBTQ+ movement, at its core, has been about seeking acceptance, rights, and equality for people regardless of their sexual orientation or gender identity. However, some argue that an intense focus on the ever-expanding list of identities could detract from these overarching goals. By emphasizing individualism to its extreme, the community risks appearing divided, making it easier for detractors to dismiss or undermine their more substantial objectives. It's a challenging balance to strike—honoring individual experiences and identities while ensuring that the broader mission isn't overshadowed. Some within the community fear that if every conversation centers around labels and personal identities, it might eclipse issues like LGBTQ+ rights, workplace discrimination, or healthcare access. While it's vital to recognize and respect individual identities, it's equally crucial to ensure that these discussions augment, rather than detract from, the larger goals of the movement.

## *A Global Glance at LGBTQ+ Advocacy:*

**Exploring how various nations approach LGBTQ+ rights and the pressures of political correctness:**

The global discourse on LGBTQ+ rights is as varied as the cultures and histories of the nations themselves. In Western democracies like Canada, the United States, and much of Europe, the push for LGBTQ+ rights and acceptance has seen significant progress over the past few decades. These regions have witnessed a growing acceptance of same-sex relationships, a broader understanding of gender identities, and legislative measures to protect LGBTQ+ rights. However, the cloak of political correctness that often envelops this discourse sometimes threatens to stifle genuine conversations, with critics arguing that it hampers open debate and honest exploration of concerns. On the other end of the spectrum, numerous countries, especially in regions like Africa, the Middle East, and parts of Asia, remain staunchly conservative in their views, with laws that criminalize homosexuality and a stringent adherence to traditional gender norms. In these nations, the very mention of LGBTQ+ rights, let alone the nuances of political correctness associated with it, can be seen as a Western import, alien and incompatible with indigenous cultural values.

**Emphasizing countries that find the very notion of multiple genders and transgenderism as disconnected from their cultural or biological realities:**

While the West grapples with the complexities of gender fluidity and the rights of transgender individuals, many countries across the globe view such concepts with skepticism or outright denial. In several African nations, for instance, homosexuality is not only criminalized but the very existence of LGBTQ+ communities is often publicly denied by political leaders. Transgenderism, in these contexts, is seen as a foreign anomaly, incongruent with the dominant cultural and biological paradigms. Russia, with its "gay propaganda" law, offers another example where the state has taken measures to suppress any advocacy or even acknowledgment of LGBTQ+ realities, let alone the intricate conversations surrounding multiple gender identities. The broader sentiment in such regions is a mix of cultural preservation, religious dictates, and, often, a resistance against what's perceived as Western cultural imperialism.

**Delving into the potential pitfalls of applying Western LGBTQ+ advocacy models to non-Western cultures:**

The fight for LGBTQ+ rights, as framed in Western contexts, often runs into challenges when superimposed on non-Western cultures. The Western model, steeped in individual rights and personal freedoms, may not always resonate in cultures where communal values, traditions, and religious beliefs hold sway. For instance, the advocacy strategies employed in San Francisco or Amsterdam may be met with resistance or even backlash in Riyadh or Kampala. There's a perceived arrogance in the assumption that Western LGBTQ+ advocacy models are universally applicable. Such approaches can sometimes be viewed as neo-colonial, with Western nations attempting to impose their values on other societies. It's crucial to recognize that genuine LGBTQ+ advocacy in non-Western regions might require a deep understanding of local cultural nuances, a willingness to engage in dialogue without preconceived notions, and strategies tailored to local contexts. The one-size-fits-all approach, critics argue, is not only ineffective but potentially detrimental to the very cause it seeks to promote.

## *Forecasting the Path Ahead:*

### The Consequences of Overemphasis on Special Rights:

The journey of the LGBTQ+ movement, like many rights-based movements, began as a quest for equal treatment and freedom from discrimination. It aimed to ensure that one's sexual orientation or gender identity did not serve as barriers to the basic rights and dignities afforded to all. However, as with many causes, there's a potential pitfall when the emphasis shifts from seeking equal rights to demanding special privileges. By constantly foregrounding LGBTQ+ issues, particularly in contexts where it's not always relevant, there's a risk of creating further divisions and animosities. There's merit in the argument that continuously highlighting differences, rather than shared human experiences, can widen societal gaps instead of bridging them. It's essential to recognize that the right to equality doesn't necessarily translate to a demand for special attention or treatment.

### Prioritizing Treatment Over Special Treatment:

One of the core tenets of any rights-based movement should be the pursuit of equitable treatment. This means being treated fairly, having access to the same opportunities, and living free from discrimination. The LGBTQ+ community, undeniably, deserves these rights. However, when the narrative shifts to seeking special treatment, the essence of the movement can get clouded. For instance, instead of primarily focusing on issues like workplace discrimination against LGBTQ+ individuals, an undue emphasis on curating ultra-specific gender-neutral language for all conceivable scenarios may detract from the more pressing issues at hand. The LGBTQ+ community would be better served by campaigns that focus on tangible outcomes like equal pay, protection from hate crimes, and access to healthcare, rather than being embroiled in debates about minutiae that the broader public may find esoteric or even alienating.

**Embracing Privacy and Reducing Overexposure:**

While it's crucial to live authentically and be true to oneself, there's also value in discretion and privacy, particularly in personal matters. Every individual, regardless of their sexual orientation or gender identity, has aspects of their lives they choose to keep private. Just as heterosexual individuals might not disclose every detail of their personal relationships or choices at work or in social situations, it's worth questioning why anyone should feel compelled to overexpose their personal life, especially when it comes to one's sexual orientation or gender identity. By making private aspects of life unduly public, there's a risk of perpetuating stereotypes or continually spotlighting differences. A focus on common human goals, shared aspirations, and mutual respect might pave the way for a more cohesive and harmonious society.

# Chapter 14
# Transgender Women in Women's Sports:
# The Quest for Fairness

## *The Rise of Transgender Participation*

### Tracing the Historical Trajectory of Transgender Women's Participation in Women's Sports

The participation of transgender women in women's sports is a relatively recent phenomenon in the vast timeline of organized athletics. Historically, sports have been divided along binary lines, purely on the basis of biological sex. However, with evolving understandings of gender and recognition of transgender rights, there has been a push for inclusivity. In the last few decades, international sports bodies, such as the International Olympic Committee (IOC), began establishing guidelines for the inclusion of transgender athletes. For example, the IOC in 2004 established that transgender women could compete in the women's category provided they had undergone gender confirmation surgery and had been on hormone therapy for a specific duration.

Yet, this journey was not smooth. It was marked with several challenges, most notably concerning the fairness of competition. Many questioned whether transgender women, even after transitioning, held any residual physical advantages over women, making the competition uneven. The debate around this issue became especially pronounced in cases where transgender women began securing top spots in various sporting events.

**Outlining the Associated Controversies and Societal Debates that Emerged**

As transgender women athletes began to make their mark, multiple controversies erupted. A notable example is the case of Rachel McKinnon, a Canadian transgender cyclist who won the UCI Masters Track World Championship in 2018. McKinnon's victory led to a storm of debate, with some competitors and commentators questioning the fairness of her participation. Cases like McKinnon's brought forth two primary contentions: the physiological advantages of transgender women and the potential undermining of women's sports.

One of the significant points of contention has been about the potential physical advantages that transgender women retain from male puberty, such as bone density and muscle mass, even after hormone therapy. Critics argue that such advantages, make the competition unfair to women athletes. The devil's advocate might point out that while inclusivity should be essential, there needs to be a point to ensure that the original intent of women's sports—to provide women an equitable platform to compete—is not compromised.

**Discussing the Broader Implications for Women's Sports**

The participation of transgender women in women's sports has ignited a broader discussion on the very nature and purpose of segregating sports by gender. Historically, women's sports were established to give female athletes a level playing field, as they were often barred or discouraged from competing in traditionally male-dominated arenas. Now, with the inclusion of transgender women, most argue that the original intent of women's sports is under threat.

A devil's advocate might posit that if transgender women, especially those who transition after experiencing male puberty, continue to dominate in women's sports, it could demoralize women athletes. This could, in turn, reduce female participation or interest in sports. The broader implications also touch upon scholarships, sponsorships, and sports funding. If transgender women secure a disproportionate amount of these opportunities, it could lead to significant disillusionment and debate about the future trajectory of women's sports.

In this charged atmosphere, the challenge remains to ensure that sports remain a domain of fair competition and in doing so, there should be a separate category for trans-athletes.

## *Biological Considerations*

### Deep Diving into the Inherent Biological Differences Between Men and Women

It's essential to understand that male and female bodies have inherent biological differences. This isn't just about reproductive anatomy but encompasses aspects like muscle mass, bone density, lung capacity, and even the distribution of fast-twitch muscle fibers. Men, on average, have a higher percentage of lean muscle mass, larger hearts and lungs, and denser bones compared to women. These differences begin to manifest during puberty when an influx of sex-specific hormones influences body composition and development. As a result, male athletes, especially in power and endurance sports, tend to outperform their female counterparts, making mixed-gender competitions skewed in favor of male participants.

The devil's advocate perspective here could suggest that these inherent physiological advantages might give transgender women, especially those who transition post-puberty, a competitive edge in women's sports. For instance, while training, recovery, and competition intensities can vary among athletes, the biological baseline that transgender women start from might be different, and arguably more advantageous, than that of cisgender women. And they wouldn't be wrong.

**Evaluating the Potential Effects of Hormone Treatments on these Biological Differences**

Hormone treatments, which include suppressing testosterone and introducing estrogen, are a significant part of the transitioning process for many transgender women. Over time, these treatments lead to reduced muscle mass, fat redistribution, and decreased bone density. The key question here is to what extent these treatments negate the physiological advantages transgender women might have acquired during male puberty.

While hormone therapies do bring about considerable changes in the body, some argue that they might not entirely erase the benefits of male puberty. For instance, aspects like bone structure and lung capacity, which play a crucial role in certain sports, may not undergo significant change with hormone treatments. From a devil's advocate viewpoint, the bone structure, particularly the broader shoulder span and narrower hips of transgender women, might confer an advantage in sports that require upper body strength or aerodynamic form.

**Debating the Fairness of Allowing Transgender Women to Compete Based on these Considerations**

The question of fairness is at the heart of the transgender women in sports debate. If one assumes that transgender women retain certain advantages even after transitioning, it becomes a complex issue of balancing inclusivity with fairness. Most argue that the essence of sports, especially at elite levels, is to ensure a level playing field. Therefore, if any group, be it men, women, or transgender women, holds an innate advantage, it disrupts this level field.

An intelligent person would argue that while society should be accommodating and respectful of individual rights, competitive sports is not the arena for these accommodations, especially if they jeopardize the integrity of women's competitions. There's also the matter of how to measure and quantify these advantages. How does one decide what level of advantage is "acceptable"? Does a two-year hormone treatment equate to a level playing field? Or should there be other metrics in place? The answers are NO. The debate on fairness isn't just about biological considerations but also about the very ethos of competitive sports.

## *Fairness and Competitive Integrity*

### Delving into the Core Principles of Competitive Sports

Sports, particularly at the competitive and professional levels, are built on principles of fairness, merit, and equal opportunity. Athletes dedicate years, sometimes decades, of their lives to mastering their craft, undergoing grueling training regimes, and making countless sacrifices. The expectation is that when they step onto the field, court, track, or pool, they will compete on a level playing field. Everyone abides by the same rules, and the outcomes are determined purely by skill, strategy, and physical prowess. These principles are foundational because they not only ensure the integrity of the sport but also protect the rights and efforts of the athletes involved.

Taking an intelligent person's stance, one should argue that introducing competitors who might have an inherent biological advantage would disrupt this carefully constructed balance. The concern isn't about the gender identity of the competitors but about the potential physiological advantages that could stem from having experienced male puberty. And while sports have always been a space for challenging human limits, they have also been a space for ensuring that challenges are met on equal grounds.

### Analyzing How the Inclusion of Transgender Women Might Compromise the Historically Maintained Level Playing Field in Women's Sports

Women's sports, historically, have been a space for women to compete, primarily because of the broad physiological differences between the average male and female body. As discussed earlier, these differences span beyond reproductive anatomy and influence aspects vital for many sports, such as muscle mass, lung capacity, and bone density. From this viewpoint, the inclusion of transgender women, especially those who transition after puberty, raises questions about maintaining this level playing field.

Drawing from real-life examples, in recent years, there have been instances where transgender women athletes dominated in various sports competitions, sparking debate and controversy. For instance, that of transgender swimmer Lia Thomas. Originally a member of the University of Pennsylvania men's swim team, Thomas later transitioned and began competing in the women's category. Her performance was stellar, breaking multiple records. This swift change in her competitive category led many to question the fairness of such participation.

Riley Gaines, an NCAA All-American swimmer from the University of Kentucky, offers a firsthand account of the challenges and dilemmas faced by female athletes in such situations. Gaines, having tied with Thomas in a 200 freestyle race, was informed that the sole trophy would be awarded to Thomas for photographic purposes. This decision, Gaines articulated, felt like a mockery to her and other female athletes, as though their achievements were sidelined for the sake of upholding a particular narrative. She felt that the broader athletic system was prioritizing the validation of transgender athletes over the sentiments and efforts of cisgender women athletes.

Adding to the complexity of the situation, when Thomas began to use the women's locker room, many of the female athletes expressed discomfort. Despite their reservations, they felt silenced, unable to voice their concerns for fear of backlash or being labeled as transphobic. Such situations bring to light the intense pressure and the fine balance that institutions and individuals must navigate. While it's essential to support and respect the rights of transgender individuals, critics argue that this should not come at the perceived expense of the rights and comforts of cisgender women. These debates underscore the need for more comprehensive guidelines, research, and dialogue to ensure that sports remain a fair and inclusive domain for all.

## Discussing Potential Solutions to Maintain Competitive Integrity, Like Creating a Separate League for Transgenders

One solution proposed by critics is the creation of a separate league or category for transgender athletes. The idea here is to ensure that everyone has a platform to compete without compromising the principles of fairness and competitive integrity. By providing a distinct category, transgender athletes can compete without the debate of potential advantages, and cisgender women can compete with the assurance of a level playing field.

However, while on the surface, this might seem like a straightforward solution, it comes with its own set of challenges. Firstly, such a move could be seen as segregating transgender athletes, further alienating an already marginalized group. Secondly, the logistical aspects of creating and maintaining such leagues on a global scale, especially when the number of transgender athletes might be relatively small in certain regions or sports, could be daunting. Lastly, creating a separate category might inadvertently signal that transgender women are not 'real' women, perpetuating stereotypes, and misconceptions. Even from a devil's advocate viewpoint, while the idea aims to address competitive fairness, it raises essential questions about societal inclusivity and acceptance.

## *Case Studies*

### Presenting Specific Instances Where Transgender Women Have Notably Participated in Women's Sports

One of the most discussed instances in recent years involves the case of Rachel McKinnon, a transgender woman who clinched victory in the women's 35-39 age category at the 2018 UCI Masters Track Cycling World Championships. Her win was a landmark moment, not only for her personal achievements but also for being a symbol of transgender women's participation in sports at a high level. Another notable example is Fallon Fox, a transgender MMA fighter who gained significant attention due to her participation in women's MMA. Fox's matches often led to heated debates due to the physical nature of the sport and concerns about safety and fairness.

Yet another example is Laurel Hubbard, a transgender weightlifter from New Zealand who competed in the women's super-heavyweight category. Hubbard's participation in international events, particularly the Tokyo 2020 Olympics, became a focal point of discussions about the intersection of gender identity, biology, and sportsmanship. These instances, among others, have set the stage for broader discussions about transgender women's participation in women's sports.

## Analyzing Reactions from Athletes, Fans, and Sporting Bodies to These Instances

The reactions to the participation of transgender women in women's sports have been a mélange of support, concern, and outright opposition. Many athletes, especially those in direct competition with transgender participants, have expressed concerns about fairness. For instance, after McKinnon's victory, Jen Wagner-Assali, who secured third place, voiced her grievances by saying the race was "definitely NOT fair."

Sporting bodies are caught in a quagmire as they attempt to create policies that are both inclusive and uphold the principles of fairness in competition. Organizations like the International Olympic Committee (IOC) have set guidelines that allow transgender women to compete if they maintain testosterone levels below a certain threshold for a specified period. Still, these guidelines are frequently under scrutiny and debate.

Fans, on the other hand, are divided. While many cheer for the progressiveness and inclusivity demonstrated when transgender women compete, others are concerned about the future integrity of women's sports. Social media platforms often become battlegrounds of opinions, with hashtags both in support of and against the participation of transgender women trending during major sporting events.

**Debating the Broader Implications of These Cases for the Future of Women's Sports**

From a devil's advocate viewpoint, these case studies pose questions that reach far beyond individual events. There's an underlying debate about what women's sports will look like in the future. If transgender women with potential physiological advantages continue to participate and dominate, will it dissuade cisgender women from competing? Will records set by cisgender women be increasingly hard to break or even unattainable?

Furthermore, these cases place a spotlight on the sports organizations and their role in shaping the future landscape. If organizations amend their rules to be more inclusive, they risk backlash from those who believe they're compromising on competitive fairness. On the other hand, if they impose stringent rules against transgender participation, they face criticism for being exclusionary.

Lastly, the debate isn't just about sports; it's about societal perceptions and acceptance. Women's sports, historically seen as a beacon of empowerment and equal opportunity, are now at the forefront of one of the most complex and contentious debates of the 21st century. As these case studies show, the path forward is intricate, demanding a balance between inclusivity, fairness, and the ever-evolving understanding of gender identity.

## *Legal and Ethical Implications*

**Mapping the Current Legal Landscape Surrounding Transgender Women's Participation in Women's Sports**

The legal framework surrounding transgender women's participation in women's sports is complex and varies from one jurisdiction to another. In the U.S., for instance, several states have proposed or passed legislation that would restrict transgender women and girls from competing in women's sports, basing their arguments largely on perceived biological advantages. Idaho's "Fairness in Women's Sports Act" is one such example, which was signed into law in 2020. This law mandates that student-athletes compete under the sex listed on their birth certificates, effectively excluding transgender girls and women from participating in female sports leagues. The law faced immediate legal challenges and represents the contentious nature of this issue.

In contrast, other nations like Canada have more inclusive guidelines. Canada allows transgender athletes to compete in accordance with their gender identity without the need for gender-confirming surgeries. However, like the U.S., policies can vary at provincial or league levels. The European perspective is equally diverse, with countries like the UK allowing self-identification for sports participation, while others lean towards more restrictive policies.

**Analyzing How Various Countries and Sports Associations are Navigating this Issue**

Sports associations around the world are grappling with the challenge of integrating transgender athletes while preserving competitive integrity. The International Olympic Committee (IOC), for instance, has guidelines in place that transgender women can compete in women's events provided they have declared that their gender identity is female and that their testosterone levels have remained below a certain threshold for at least 12 months. However, this too is not without contention, with many pointing out potential flaws or ambiguities in the guidelines.

The NCAA, governing collegiate sports in the U.S., has a similar policy, emphasizing a testosterone suppression threshold. However, individual states with restrictive laws are in direct conflict with these guidelines, creating a patchwork of rules that athletes, coaches, and administrators must navigate.

In Australia, the Australian Sports Commission and the National Sports Federation have jointly issued guidelines that are more inclusive, focusing on discrimination prevention. The guidelines discourage unnecessary medical interventions and focus on creating a safe and inclusive environment for all athletes, including transgender and gender-diverse individuals.

**Discussing the Ethical Dimensions, Weighing Individual Rights Against Collective Fairness**

From an ethical standpoint, the inclusion of transgender women in female sports touches upon the deeply entrenched values of fairness, inclusivity, and individual rights. On one hand, there's an argument for the rights of transgender individuals to be recognized and respected, allowing them to compete in accordance with their gender identity. Denying them this right can be viewed as discriminatory, perpetuating the marginalization and stigmatization they already face in many facets of society.

Conversely, from a devil's advocate viewpoint, there's a compelling argument surrounding the sanctity of a level playing field in sports. Many assert that regardless of gender identity, biological differences provide transgender women with undeniable advantages in certain sports, thereby undermining the principles of fair competition. This argument posits that the inclusion of transgender women could potentially jeopardize opportunities, scholarships, and accolades for cisgender female athletes.

Navigating this ethical minefield requires a delicate balance. While the right to identity and participation is paramount, the essence of sports—a fair competition where participants are adjudged based on skill, strategy, and effort, rather than inherent physiological advantages—should not be overshadowed.

## *The Athletes' Perspective*

### Capturing the Viewpoints of Female Athletes

The debate surrounding transgender women's participation in women's sports is especially poignant for female athletes who are directly affected by these decisions. Many have voiced their opinions, falling largely into two camps. Martina Navratilova, an 18-time Grand Slam tennis champion and gay rights advocate, has been one of the most vocal opponents. She has argued that allowing transgender women to compete against women is "insane and cheating," citing the potential physiological advantages. On the other end of the spectrum are voices like Megan Rapinoe, a professional soccer player, who argues in favor of inclusivity and the fundamental rights of transgender athletes.

Between these prominent voices lies a myriad of opinions. While some athletes express fears about the potential erosion of opportunities and the essence of fair competition, others emphasize empathy, understanding, and the importance of sports as a unifying force that should be accessible to everyone, regardless of gender identity.

### Debating the Potential Long-Term Negative Implications on Women's Sports

From a devil's advocate perspective, the long-term ramifications of allowing transgender women to compete in women's sports are concerning for most. The primary worry is that the essence of competitive sports, rooted in a level playing field, might be distorted. If transgender women, with perceived physiological advantages, start to dominate certain sports, the narrative could shift from skill, training, and athleticism to biological differences, undermining the achievements of female athletes.

Moreover, there's a concern about the potential dwindling of opportunities for women. Scholarships, sponsorships, and even selection for teams could be at stake if transgender women begin to outperform their female counterparts consistently. Such a trend could disincentivize women from pursuing sports, leading to decreased participation and potentially stunting the growth of women's sports.

## Discussing Potential Compromises or Solutions that Cater to All Athletes' Concerns

Finding a middle ground in this charged debate is no easy feat, but some potential compromises have been proposed. One idea is to establish a separate category or league for transgender athletes. This would ensure that transgender athletes have a platform to compete while also maintaining the competitive integrity of cisgender women's sports. However, this proposal is not without its critics, as it may further marginalize transgender athletes and create logistical challenges.

Another approach involves refining guidelines about hormone levels. Ensuring that transgender women maintain specific testosterone levels for an extended period before competing could level the playing field. This is already being implemented by organizations like the IOC, but the optimal levels and duration are subjects of ongoing research and debate.

Lastly, some argue for a more individualistic assessment, where factors like age of transition, hormone levels, training history, and specific physiological parameters are taken into account to determine eligibility. While complex, such an approach would attempt to consider the nuances and individual differences that blanket policies might overlook.

## *Looking Ahead*

**Projecting the Negative Future Landscape of Women's Sports with Growing Transgender Participation**

From a "devil's advocate" standpoint, critics argue that if the current trajectory of transgender participation in women's sports continues unchecked, the very essence of women's sports might be at risk. In this potential future, as more transgender women with perceived physiological advantages begin to dominate the podiums, the narrative could shift from celebrating talent and hard work to a dialogue centered around biological discrepancies. Such a landscape could diminish the hard-won accomplishments of female athletes, painting their achievements under the shadow of the transgender debate. There might be a consequent erosion of interest in women's sports from both spectators and sponsors if competitions are perceived as imbalanced. For instance, the victories of Fallon Fox, a transgender MMA fighter, were met with controversy and claims that her successes were solely due to her biological advantages, overshadowing her skills and training.

**Outlining Potential Challenges that Await**

With an evolving sports landscape, several challenges loom on the horizon. One primary concern is the potential for a "brain drain" from women's sports. If female athletes begin to feel that they're consistently at a disadvantage, there could be a decrease in participation rates, leading to a potential decline in the talent pool. This could be especially pronounced in sports where physical strength and size play pivotal roles.

Moreover, there's the legal quagmire. Lawsuits could arise from athletes who feel they've been unjustly sidelined in favor of transgender competitors. An example can be drawn from Connecticut, where a group of high school athletes filed a lawsuit after losing to two transgender sprinters. Such legal battles could drain resources from sporting bodies, lead to negative publicity, and further polarize the community.

Lastly, a more intangible yet equally important challenge is the potential deterioration of camaraderie and unity within teams and the broader sporting community. If athletes are divided over the issue, team dynamics could suffer, leading to reduced performance and cohesion.

**Proposing Recommendations for Ensuring Fairness, Inclusivity, and Competitive Integrity in the Future**

One key recommendation is extensive research. Understanding the precise physiological impacts of transitioning, especially with hormone treatments, can offer clearer insights into any potential advantages or disadvantages. This research should be continuous, as medical technologies and techniques evolve.

Another proposal is to emphasize transparency and dialogue. Sporting bodies should be transparent in their decision-making processes and be open to feedback. Athlete councils, comprising cisgender and transgender athletes, can be created to ensure all voices are represented in decision-making processes.

Lastly, a more futuristic solution could involve technological interventions. As sports technology advances, there could be ways to quantify and potentially level out any physiological advantages. Wearable tech, for instance, might provide data-driven insights into an athlete's capabilities, allowing for more informed decisions regarding categorizations and competitions. While potentially controversial, such a data-driven approach could be a way forward in an increasingly complex sporting world.

# Conclusion
# From Understanding to Action

## *Recapitulating the Journey*

### Reflecting on the Origins of Political Correctness and its Evolution Over Time

The roots of political correctness trace back to earnest desires to cultivate a society of understanding, inclusivity, and mutual respect. The initial intent was to redress historical wrongs and protect marginalized groups from verbal harm. Over time, what began as a righteous campaign to foster inclusivity and discourage discriminatory language transformed into a convoluted web of linguistic gymnastics. Cultural lexicons began changing rapidly, often making it challenging to keep up with what was deemed appropriate. For instance, the term 'political correctness' itself, which started as a sincere initiative, was co-opted by critics as a pejorative to highlight its perceived excesses. The progression of political correctness was not linear. As society evolved, so did the understanding and application of these terms and ideologies.

### Discussing the Nuances, Few Benefits, and Many Drawbacks of This Cultural Phenomenon

While political correctness aimed at safeguarding minority rights and curbing discriminatory speech, it also inadvertently bred a culture of silence in some spheres. Its benefits are evident in the heightened societal awareness and empathy towards historically marginalized groups. The dialogue surrounding racism, sexism, and other forms of discrimination has undoubtedly advanced, leading to a more informed and compassionate society.

However, its drawbacks are plenty. The "devil's advocate" would argue that the overzealous application of political correctness has suppressed free speech, limited artistic creativity, and curtailed genuine discourse. People became increasingly cautious, fearing backlash over unintentional linguistic missteps. For example, comedians began self-censoring their content, concerned about the repercussions of offending certain groups. In academia, scholars hesitated to explore certain topics, apprehensive of being labeled insensitive or worse. This culture of fear and self-censorship could, in the long run, stifle progress and open discourse, ironically creating a society where people feel more divided and misunderstood.

## Revisiting Pivotal Moments and Discussions from the Book, Such as the Debate Surrounding Transgender Women in Sports

One of the most heated discussions in the contemporary landscape of political correctness is the inclusion of transgender women in women's sports. This issue, dissected in depth in a prior chapter, epitomizes the challenges of balancing individual rights with collective fairness. On one hand, the push for inclusivity demands that transgender women be allowed to compete in women's categories. On the other, concerns about biological differences and competitive integrity cast shadows over such inclusion.

This debate underscores the broader challenges posed by political correctness. It brings to the forefront the question: At what point does the push for inclusivity compromise fairness or the original intent of an institution, such as women's sports? Instances like these compel society to introspect deeply, challenging our understanding of rights, fairness, and equality in a constantly evolving world. As with many discussions in this book, there are no easy answers, only complex considerations and the ongoing pursuit of a balanced perspective.

## *Reclaiming Conversation*

### The Imperativeness of Fostering Open Dialogue in an Increasingly Polarized Society

In recent years, society has grown alarmingly polarized, with people clustering into ideologically homogeneous groups. Such polarization is detrimental to societal progress and understanding. Political correctness, in its more extreme form, has inadvertently fostered this divide. By curbing open discourse and punishing those who deviate from the accepted narrative, society risks creating an environment where individuals are more likely to retreat into their ideological enclaves, shutting out opposing viewpoints. But fostering open dialogue is paramount in stitching together the fraying fabric of society. Open conversations lead to mutual respect, understanding, and often, compromise. They lay the foundation for a society where differences are discussed, not suppressed. Historically, every major societal shift, whether in civil rights, women's rights, or other social justice movements, began with open dialogues that questioned the status quo.

### Emphasizing the Importance of Understanding Diverse Perspectives While Holding Onto One's Beliefs and Principles and Not Giving Into Political Pressure from Society at Large

One of the significant critiques against extreme political correctness is the perceived pressure it exerts on individuals to conform to a particular way of thinking. While understanding and respecting diverse perspectives is a laudable goal, individuals must not feel compelled to relinquish their core beliefs and principles due to societal pressure. For instance, one might read about a professor who faced backlash for not adopting new gender-neutral pronouns, not out of disrespect, but because they believed the rapid changes in language were eroding linguistic clarity. Such individuals should be allowed space in society to express their beliefs without fear of retribution. Authentic understanding comes from engaging with these differing views, not by suppressing them. The "devil's advocate" would argue that political correctness, in its overzealousness, sometimes risks overshadowing the foundational values of free speech and individual liberty.

## Highlighting the Potential Dangers of Echo Chambers and Emphasizing the Value of Engaging with Differing Viewpoints

Echo chambers, facilitated by modern technology and social media algorithms, are spaces where individuals are only exposed to viewpoints that align with their own. These chambers reinforce existing beliefs and shut out opposing perspectives. While they provide comfort and validation, they are breeding grounds for extremism and misinformation. For instance, one could cite the rise of several online communities that propagate conspiracy theories; members of these communities rarely interact with opposing views, leading to an intensified belief in the conspiracy. Extreme political correctness, by discouraging diverse viewpoints, can inadvertently contribute to the creation of these echo chambers. Engaging with differing opinions, even if they challenge our core beliefs, is essential for personal growth and societal progress. It forces individuals to reassess and strengthen their convictions and fosters a society where ideas compete, and the best ones thrive.

## *Beyond the Book*

## The Role and Responsibility of Readers in Today's Age: To Be Active Contributors to Discourse, Not Just Passive Consumers

The role of a reader has evolved with the advent of the digital age. Gone are the days when individuals were mere recipients of information, limited to newspapers and television broadcasts. Today's digital platforms offer everyone a podium, turning readers into contributors, amplifiers, and even detractors of information. Yet, with this power comes immense responsibility. For every online debate that seeks to understand, countless others degrade into name-calling and unfounded accusations. The criticism of political correctness often arises from instances where individuals face disproportionate backlash for expressing contrarian views. For instance, one might recall instances of online "cancel culture" where individuals faced severe repercussions for minor infractions or misinterpretations. Readers, now participants in the discourse, need to understand the weight of their words and actions. Instead of joining the fray mindlessly, they should strive to be discerning contributors, promoting genuine understanding rather than division.

## Encouraging Readers to Challenge Themselves, to Seek Out and Understand Perspectives Different from Their Own

If there's one thing that this book hopes to achieve, it's to inspire readers to go beyond their comfort zones. In a world swayed by political correctness, there's an all too familiar temptation to nod along with popular opinion, to retweet the trending hashtag without delving deeper. But genuine growth, both personal and societal, requires challenging oneself. An example that comes to mind is a university student who, despite being a staunch progressive, decided to attend a series of conservative seminars to better understand their arguments. By the end, while her fundamental beliefs remained unchanged, she gained respect for some conservative concerns and was better equipped to debate them. Such endeavors promote understanding, dispelling stereotypes, and building bridges in a polarized world. Readers are encouraged to read contrarian views, listen to podcasts that challenge their beliefs, and engage in conversations where they're not the majority voice.

## Highlighting the Importance of Free Expression and Standing Up for Respect, Emphasizing that the Two Are Not Mutually Exclusive

The crux of the debate surrounding political correctness often boils down to a perceived trade-off between free expression and respect. Detractors argue that in the quest to be overly respectful, society is curbing genuine expression. However, one can advocate for free speech while still promoting respect and understanding. An example that epitomizes this is the case of a renowned journalist who, while interviewing a controversial figure, managed to ask tough, probing questions without resorting to mockery or disdain. Such instances demonstrate that it's entirely possible to maintain a civil discourse without sacrificing the tenets of free expression. Respect doesn't necessitate the silencing of voices; it simply requires that disagreements be aired thoughtfully. As readers and contributors to the global conversation, individuals have the power to reshape discourse, emphasizing that respect and free expression can, and should, coexist.

## *Envisioning a Balanced Future*

**Imagining a World Where Individual Rights are Safeguarded Without Compromising Collective Fairness**

One of the central criticisms of political correctness, as this book has underscored, is the perceived tension between individual rights and collective fairness. Historically, societies have always grappled with striking this balance. In our quest to protect individual rights, especially the right to free speech, are we inadvertently trampling upon collective fairness? Consider, for instance, the contentious debates in many Western universities over controversial guest speakers. While some argue for the absolute right of these speakers to share their views, others feel that allowing certain controversial figures a platform could perpetuate harm and misinformation. However, envision a future where universities, as citadels of free thought, uphold individual rights by allowing such speakers, but simultaneously ensure collective fairness by organizing counter-speeches or debates that expose students to multiple viewpoints. Such an environment doesn't suppress voices; instead, it amplifies a chorus of diverse opinions, promoting a holistic understanding.

## The Dream of a Society That Ensures No One is Silenced, Yet Everyone Feels Heard and Respected

The dream of an ideal society is one where the pendulum doesn't swing to extremes—where the concerns about political correctness don't mean stifling expression, but rather fostering an environment of mutual respect. For instance, there's an anecdote about a town hall meeting in a small community. When a controversial issue arose, instead of suppressing dissenting opinions in the name of political correctness, the organizers set ground rules that promoted respectful dialogue. Participants were encouraged to speak their minds but were also reminded to listen actively and avoid personal attacks. By the meeting's end, while not everyone agreed, they left with a deeper understanding of opposing viewpoints. The dream for our broader society is similar: a space where disagreements aren't just tolerated but are actively encouraged, provided they are framed within the bounds of respect.

## Discussing Potential Steps Society Can Take to Move Towards This Balanced Vision

Achieving this balanced vision is neither simple nor immediate, but there are actionable steps societies can take. First, educational institutions can play a pivotal role. By introducing curricula that prioritize critical thinking, debate, and the exploration of diverse viewpoints, students can be equipped to navigate complex discussions without resorting to the silencing tactics often associated with extreme political correctness. Secondly, media organizations can strive for more balanced reportage. By actively seeking out diverse voices and avoiding echo chambers, they can foster more nuanced public discussions. Lastly, on an individual level, people can actively seek out interactions and information sources that challenge their existing beliefs. Whether this involves attending a seminar, reading a contrarian article, or simply engaging in a conversation with someone of a different viewpoint, such endeavors can chip away at the divisive barriers that extreme political correctness has sometimes unintentionally erected.

## *The Role of Education and Media*

**Reiterating the Importance of Educational Institutions and Media in Shaping Societal Perceptions and Beliefs for the Betterment of Society and Not the Whims of the Elite**

Education and media have always been foundational pillars in the development and dissemination of societal beliefs. Historically, these institutions have acted as the gatekeepers of information, guiding populations through eras of war, peace, innovation, and societal change. However, in recent times, there's been growing concern that these institutions are becoming heavily influenced by political correctness, often shaped by a select few elites. Take, for instance, the case of certain historical figures being "canceled" in textbooks due to their controversial pasts. While it's vital to recognize and rectify historical wrongs, eliminating them from curricula might rob students of the opportunity to critically evaluate the complexities of these figures. Such editorial decisions, often influenced by a handful of people, can have ripple effects on how entire generations perceive their history.

**Emphasizing Their Role in Fostering Critical Thinking, Discernment, and Empathy Among Populations**

While political correctness has its roots in the pursuit of respect and understanding, an extreme application in educational and media contexts might unintentionally stifle critical thinking. Education, at its core, should challenge students, prompting them to question, debate, and arrive at their own conclusions. Media, similarly, should present facts, differing viewpoints, and nuanced analyses, enabling the public to make informed decisions. A pertinent example can be drawn from a university where students protested the reading of a classic literary work, citing its "problematic" themes. While the concerns of the students were valid, an outright ban deprived them of the opportunity to dissect, discuss, and understand the context of the work. Instead, educational institutions can incorporate such contentious materials but frame them with appropriate context, fostering discernment and empathy.

## Discussing Potential Reforms and Initiatives to Ensure a More Informed and Understanding Society

Navigating the tightrope of political correctness in education and media demands reforms that emphasize balance. Firstly, curricula and media content should be co-created with a diverse group of stakeholders, ensuring multiple perspectives are considered, rather than a singular dominant narrative. Schools and universities might establish review boards comprising educators, students, and community members to evaluate and recommend materials. In the media realm, organizations can prioritize diversity in their editorial boards, ensuring varied voices shape the content.

Another reform could be the introduction of media literacy programs in schools, equipping students to discern biases, recognize credible sources, and understand the complexities of narratives. This would aid in immunizing them against the perils of fake news and extreme viewpoints.

Lastly, both sectors can proactively foster environments where questioning is encouraged. Whether it's a classroom debate or a town hall facilitated by a media house, creating spaces where individuals can discuss, dissent, and deliberate will pave the way for a society that values both respect and free expression.

# Calls to Action

**Concrete Steps and Initiatives Readers Can Undertake in Their Personal, Professional, and Societal Lives to Promote Understanding, Respect, and Balanced Discourse**

At the personal level, readers can begin by introspecting and identifying any unconscious biases they may hold. It's not enough to passively reject extreme political correctness; active self-improvement can set the stage for genuine understanding. One could engage with literature, films, or other cultural artifacts from diverse sources, thus broadening their horizons and dismantling stereotypical perceptions. For example, instead of avoiding or protesting a book for its "problematic" content, readers can critically engage with it, forming a balanced viewpoint.

In professional settings, individuals can advocate for training programs that emphasize genuine inclusivity and respect, as opposed to mere tokenism often driven by excessive political correctness. In a business scenario, for instance, instead of merely celebrating diversity-themed days, organizations can host regular workshops to tackle deep-rooted biases and promote genuine conversation.

In the wider society, engaging with community programs, attending public lectures, and participating in events that foster cross-cultural interactions can pave the way for understanding. These initiatives help individuals break out of their echo chambers, encouraging them to encounter and empathize with diverse perspectives.

**The Importance of Grassroots Movements and Community Dialogues in Driving Societal Change**

Grassroots movements play an unparalleled role in driving genuine societal change. Such movements, emerging from the ground up, are typically more in tune with the needs and concerns of the average individual, compared to top-down initiatives which might be disconnected from on-ground realities. Remember the backlash against cancel culture? While a major segment of it was driven by celebrities and influential personalities, it gained momentum due to the grassroots efforts of ordinary people who felt that extreme political correctness was becoming stifling.

Community dialogues, too, play a pivotal role in this endeavor. By creating a platform where members from varied backgrounds can discuss and debate issues openly, these dialogues cut through the noise of polarized media narratives. A town in the Midwest, for example, tackled rising community tensions by hosting weekly dialogues where members could air grievances, ask questions, and find common ground. Over time, such efforts can change the fabric of society, emphasizing understanding over division.

### Encouraging Readers to Be Proactive in Their Communities, Advocating for Positive Change Based on the Principles Discussed in the Book

Being a passive observer in the face of societal shifts is not an option for readers who truly understand the dangers of unchecked political correctness. It's imperative to channel knowledge into action. Readers can start by organizing or attending discussion groups in their local communities, focusing on contentious topics and promoting balanced, respectful discourse. Libraries, community centers, or even private residences can serve as venues for such gatherings.

Furthermore, individuals can collaborate with local schools and colleges, proposing curricula that foster critical thinking and open dialogue. By actively interacting with the younger generation, readers can help mold a future that values balance and respect over extreme narratives.

Lastly, for those who witness instances where political correctness threatens genuine respect and understanding, it's vital to stand up. This might involve writing to local newspapers, supporting organizations that champion free speech, or even running for local offices to drive systemic change. After all, positive change often begins with the proactive efforts of a dedicated few.

## *A Final Word of Hope*

### Acknowledging the Challenges Ahead but Emphasizing the Potential for Positive Change

The journey towards a more balanced society, free from the shackles of extreme political correctness, will undoubtedly be fraught with challenges. As society evolves, new issues emerge, each bringing its own set of complexities. However, it's essential to approach these challenges not with trepidation, but with the understanding that they present opportunities for growth, enlightenment, and unity. The excessive tilt towards political correctness is, in many ways, a reaction to real issues of discrimination and inequity. While the response might have swung to an extreme, it underscores the genuine desire for a more inclusive society. And where there's a desire for positive change, there's potential to channel it in constructive ways.

### Inspiring Readers with Real-World Examples of Communities and Societies that Have Successfully Navigated Contentious Issues Without Reverting to Political Correctness

Around the world, numerous communities have grappled with divisive issues, without resorting to the blanket silencing that extreme political correctness often advocates. Take the example of a small town in Scandinavia. Faced with rising tensions between native residents and a growing immigrant population, town leaders initiated community dialogue sessions. Instead of suppressing contentious views, they encouraged open discussion, bridging gaps of misunderstanding through communication. The town, over time, became a beacon of harmonious coexistence, proving that genuine dialogue trumps enforced silence.

Similarly, after a divisive political event in a Southeast Asian nation, rather than stifle dissent, the government set up "Reconciliation Booths" across cities. These were spaces where citizens could openly discuss their grievances and concerns with officials, leading to more informed policy-making and a healing process for the nation.

**Leaving Readers with a Message of Hope, Unity, and the Belief that Understanding and Action Can Lead to a Brighter, More Inclusive Future**

Despite the challenges, there lies ahead a promising horizon, one where dialogue, understanding, and mutual respect illuminate the path. Societies have, time and again, demonstrated an incredible ability to adapt, evolve, and grow. While the present moment might seem dominated by divisive voices, it's crucial to remember that history is replete with instances where unity has triumphed over division.

Readers must carry forth with the belief that every conversation they initiate, every bias they challenge, and every bridge they build contributes to this brighter future. A future where the next generation won't be burdened with the tightrope walk of political correctness, but will instead breathe in an atmosphere of genuine respect and understanding. Let's envisage a world where every voice matters, where understanding isn't forced but organically cultivated, and where society thrives on the bedrock of mutual respect. It's not just a dream; with concerted effort, it's a tangible reality within grasp.